ANXIETY
IN RELATIONSHIP

The New Up-to-Date Guide for Modern Couples. How to Turn Conflicts Into Closeness and Overcome Jealousy, Insecurity, and Attachment to Develop Real Trusted Relationships

ABIGAIL MARSHALL

© **Copyright Abigail Marshall 2022 - All rights reserved.**

The content contained within this book may not be reproduced, duplicated or transmitted without direct written permission from the author or the publisher.

Under no circumstances will any blame or legal responsibility be held against the publisher, or author, for any damages, reparation, or monetary loss due to the information contained within this book. Either directly or indirectly.

Legal Notice:

This book is copyright protected. This book is only for personal use. You cannot amend, distribute, sell, use, quote or paraphrase any part, or the content within this book, without the consent of the author or publisher.

Disclaimer Notice:

By reading this document, the reader agrees that under no circumstances is the author responsible for any losses, direct or indirect, which are incurred as a result of the use of information contained within this document, including, but not limited to, — errors, omissions, or inaccuracies.

TABLE OF CONTENTS

Preface 1

Chapter 1: Introduction To Relationships And Anxiety In Relationships 4

   Types of Relationships 5

      Codependent Relationships 5

      Independent Relationships 6

      Dominant-Submissive Relationships 7

      Open Relationships 8

      Long-Distance Relationships 8

   The Stages of Relationships 8

      Merging Stage 9

      The Doubt and Denial Stage 14

      The Partnership Stage 15

   Signs of Tensions In The Relationship 16

      Physical Tiredness 16

      Always Angry With Each Other 16

      Emotional Unavailability 17

      Forgetting The Tuning 17

      Constant Dissatisfaction 18

      Over-Analysis of Relationship 18

      Low Self-Esteem 19

      Pessimism 19

      Attraction Towards Other People 19

      Wanting To Spend More Time On The Phone 20

      Overly Critical of Your Partner 21

Admittance And Attempts To Resolve Anxiety 22
    Attempts To Resolve Anxiety 23

Chapter 2: The Reasons And Manifestations Of Anxiety In A Relationship 24
    Trust Loss 25
    Vulnerability To Another Person.. 26
    Constant Comparison 26
    Lack of Communication 27
    Too Many Distractions 28
    Constant Complaining Behavior... 29
    Physical Distance.. 29
    The Spontaneity Paradox 30
    Psychological Insecurities 31
    Doubting The Feelings of Your Partner 32
    Feeling The Loss of Charm 32
    Victimization 33
    The False Expectation of Mind-Reading........................... 33
    Not Knowing Low Spots 34
    Imbalance of Financial Responsibility 35
    Careless Attitude... 35

Manifestation of Anxiety 36

Chapter 3: Start Bridging The Gap.. 39
    Get Closer To Your Partner 41
    Try To Be Understanding.. 41
        Conflicts Of Values 43
    Support Your Partner 44
        A Better Conversation 46
        Remember To Be Considerate... 46
        Listen Better 47
        Wait Patiently 47

More Involvement In Each Other's Lives 47
Improve Your Relationship By Planning Ahead................... 49
Creating A Special Bond 50
Little Gestures... 50
    Keep The Door Wide Open... 52
    Make The First Move 52
    Sending Flowers.. 53
    Creative Gift Ideas 53
    Surprise Your Partner With A Memory Book.................. 54

Chapter 4: Do Not Smother Each Other 55
Too Much Closeness Has A Negative Impact 58
    Emotionally Abusive Relationship................................... 59
    Losing Yourself In A Relationship................................... 59
    Isolating Your Partner 60
    Controlling Partner.. 60
    Being Too Reliant 60
Giving Space... 61
    Allow Each Other To Be Alone 62
    Spend Some Time Apart From Each Other...................... 62
Respect Their Privacy 63
    Private Discussions 65
    Private Emails 65
    Contacts with Third Parties 65
A Little Emotional Independence 66

Chapter 5: Relationship Counseling 69
Finding The Point When Problems Began 70
Giving Up The Ego And Forgetting The Past 72
Forgiveness of The Mistakes.. 73
Working On Weak Areas 74

Professional Relationship Counseling 75
   History of Relationship Counseling 76
   How Couples Counseling Saves A Relationship 77
   Steps To Saving A Relationship by Professional
   Counseling 80

Chapter 6: Understanding The Importance of Communication 83

   What Is Proper Communication In A Relationship? 86
      Verbal Communication 87
      Non-Verbal Communication 88
   Clean Communication 88
      Express Empathy to Your Partner 89
      Be Respectful Of Your Partner 89
      Don't Get Angry 90
      Be Truthful 90
      Jumping To Conclusions 90
   Commandments Of Communication 91
   Communication Problems 92
      Failure To Listen Or Ineffective Listening 94
      A Lack Of Deference 95
   Listening To Your Partner In A Relationship 95
      Be A Good Listener 96
      Pay Attention 97
      Giving Your Partner Space To Speak 97
   Listening 98
   History 99
   Listening Blocks 102
      Mind Reading 102
      Filtering 103
      Judging 104

Daydreaming 105
Sparring 106
Being Right 107

Strategies for Overcoming Listening Blocks 108

Pay Attention To One Another 108
Take Some Time To Pamper Yourself 108

Psychological Impact of Listening 108
Active Listening 110
Reciprocal Communication 112
Ways For Improving Communication 114

Be Forthright And Truthful 114
Be Courteous And Respectful 115
Communicate Your Emotions 115

Chapter 7: Express Your Feelings and Needs 117

Realization of Various Feelings in A Relationship 119

Respect Yourself 120
Don't Accept Anything Below What You're Worth 120
Love Is Compassionate 121
Love Is Patient 121
Love is Selfless 121

Express Your Feelings 122

Consider What You Truly Desire 123
Do Not Become Enraged Easily 123
Recognize The Importance Of Your Relationship
To You 123
Frequently Share Photos And Videos 124
Script Your Needs 124

Scrutinize Overburdening Feelings And Needs 126
Conveying Your Feelings To Your Partner 128
Find Out Your Partner's Needs 130

Make Your Partner Comfortable With Expressing Feelings 132

Chapter 8: Changing Your Aversive Strategies 135

   Eight Aversive Strategies 137

      Discounting 137

      Withdrawal 138

      Threats 139

      Blaming 140

      Belittling/Denigrating 141

      Guilt-Tripping 141

      Derailing 142

      Taking Away 143

   The Harms Of Aversive Strategies 143

      The Cold Effect Of Humiliation 144

      Loss of Connection 144

      Loss of Trust 145

      Long-Lasting Scars 145

      End of A Relationship 146

   Identification Of Aversive Behavior 146

      Disregarding 147

      Threatening 148

      Criticizing 148

      Controlling By Fear And Shame 148

      Ignorance 149

   Changing Aversive Behavior 149

Chapter 9: Anger Management 152

   How Anger Affects A Relationship 153

   History 155

   Keep Track Of Your Anger 157

   Note The Triggers 159

Thoughts for the Day 160
Distorted Thoughts 160

Combat The Blamers 161

Don't Take A Defensive Stance 162
Attempt To Comprehend The Blamer's Underlying
Issues 163

Stress Inoculation 163
Self-Instruction 165

Instruct Yourself To Unwind 166
Assure Yourself That You Can Handle The Situation ... 166
Listen To Music 167
Wear Relaxing Clothing 167
Take A Hot Shower 167
Work Out 167

Cope With The Anger Of Your Partner 167

Recognize It 168
Accept That Rage Is A Natural Emotion 168
Keep Your Cool 169
Listen 169
Recognize Your Emotions 169
Identify The Triggers Of Your Partner 170
Your Attitudes Towards The Anger Of Your Partner 171
Practice Assertive Responses 173

Probe The Criticism 174
Acknowledge The Mistakes 176
Deflect 177
Limit The Damage 179

Chapter 10: The Harm Of "Shoulds" 181

What Is The Concept Of "Shoulds"? 184
The Personal Responsibility Principle 185

    Your Partner Is Too Dependent On You 186
    To Handle Relationship Disagreements 187
    Pulling Your Relationship Out of a Rut........................... 187
    To Handle Conflicts... 188

  Six Steps Of Personal Responsibility 188

Chapter 11: Time-Outs 191

  Determine The Cause For Your Need For A Time-Out 194

  Theoretical Background 195

  History 197

  Agree On A Timeout Signal 198

  The Early Warning Signal 201

  Make Rules For Time-Outs 202

    Possible Time-Out Locations 203
    What You Should Expect During Time-Outs 203
    Move On From The Forum Wars 203
    A Time-Out Chair 204
    Truth About Time-Out 204
    A Time-Out Clock 204

  Practice The Time-Outs 205

Chapter 12: The Role of Emotional Intelligence 207

  The Impact Of The Lack Of Emotional Intelligence 209

    Recognize Your Partner's Emotions 210
    Use Your Emotions Appropriately 210

  Handling Your Emotions 211

    Handle Your Own Emotions First 211
    Be Mindful Of The Reasons Behind Your Feelings 212
    Accept Responsibility For Your Emotions 212
    Recognize The Distinction Between Being Bothered
    And Being Furious 213
    Acquire Emotional Intelligence 213

Recognize Your Emotions.. 214
Investigate Your Feeling 214
Translate Your Feelings into Words............................. 215
Manage Your Negative Emotions 215

Practice Empathy 215
Differentiate Sympathy From Empathy 217

Self-Regulation And Emotional Intelligence 219
Handling Your Partner's Emotions 222

Chapter 13: Self-Disclosure And Trust............................... 224

Be Open Mutually.. 225
Develop Your Relationship.. 226
Accept Each Other's Past 228
Be The Source Of Confidence 229
The Effect Of Different Factors On The Extent Of Self-
Disclosure 230
How Does Self-Disclosure Bridge The Gap? 232

Chapter 14: Non-Verbal Communication 234

What Is Non-Verbal Communication?................................. 234
The Effect Of Non-Verbal Communication On Couple's
Psychology... 237
What Can You Do?.. 240
Steady Eye Contact 240
Showing Emotion And Care.. 240
Keep The Focus On Your Partner While Talking 241
Touch And Its Emotional Impact On Relieving Anxiety
In A Relationship 241
Do Some Chores, Like Cooking Or Cleaning, For
Your Partner 242

Improving Non-Verbal Communication 242
Self-Awareness.. 243

    Try To Immerse Yourself In A New Culture.................. 243
    Refine Your Non-Verbal Communication...................... 243
    Body Language Should Be Affirmative 244

  How Does It Treat Anxiety And Mistrust? 244
  Face-To-Face Communication Relies On Seven Channels Of Nonverbal Communication 245

Chapter 15: Increasing Attachment 246

  Difference Between Positive And Negative Attachment 248
  Attachment And Strength Of Relationships 249
  Ways To Increase Attachment 251

Chapter 16: Overcoming Possessiveness And Jealousy 254

  Psychology of Jealousy And Possessiveness 256
  Overcome Complexes And Fearfulness 257
    Don't Think Of Love As A Reward 257
    Try Not To Be Too Charming 258

  Heal Trust Issues 258
    Find The Root of The Issue 259
    Develop Realistic Expectations 260
    Show Gratitude 261
    Accept Yourself 262

  How Can You Treat The Possessiveness Of Your Partner? 263
    Respect Your Spouse 264
    Use Caution 264

Chapter 17: Trust In A Relationship 265

  The Importance Of Trust 267
  The Meaning Of Trust In A Relationship 268
  Ways To Build Trust 270

Respectfully Treat Your Spouse 270
Be Truthful With Your Partner 270
Participate In Your Partner's Hobbies And Interests 271
How Cheating Affects A Relationship 271
Restoring The Trust 272
Discover What Caused The Trust To Be Destroyed In
The First Place 274

Chapter 18: Resolving Couple's Conflicts 276

Reasons for Conflicts 277
Unfulfilled and Unrealistic Expectations 277
Lack of Sexual Compatibility 278
Mismatched Dynamics 279
Conflict And Couples Anxiety 279
Conflict Resolution Skills for Healthy Relationships 280
Communicate Your Feelings 280
Improve your listening skills 281
Find a Solution 283
Agree to Disagree 283
Coping With Conflict 284
Is Conflict Resolution Important for Healthy
Relationships? 284

Chapter 19: Do Not Get Lost In A Relationship 287

Stay True To Yourself 289
Live With Your Values 291
Do You Believe You Have The Freedom To Be
Yourself? 292
Do You Feel Comfortable Expressing Yourself? 292
Trust Yourself 293
Pay Attention To Your Instincts 294

- Set Boundaries Because You Believe In Yourself 294
- Seek Growth 295
  - Condemning Your Spouse 295
  - Not Performing Chores 296
- Channel Your Energy Into Building A Relationship 296
  - Speak To One Another 297
  - Spend Time Together 297
  - Discover Mutual Interests 298

Conclusion 299

PREFACE

The relationships of today require more than just love to function. No human can work alone, and thus they need a life partner to share happiness and sorrows with. Love is the force that binds two humans in the bond of a relationship. But sometimes, the magic of love starts to wane, and tensions start appearing. This tension leads to anxiety in relationships.

These tensions are solvable when both partners pay attention to the causes. There is always a root cause of stress and conflict in a relationship. These become worse when none of the partners aims to resolve this anxiety.

There are so many things that maintain a healthy relationship. Love alone is not sufficient to bear the burden of a relationship. It is the main bridge in a relationship, but it needs help from other factors such as support and empathy.

The absence of support leads to misunderstandings and tensions. Neither partner is at ease when the other fails to understand and support the other. This is when anxiety creeps in, and it will only worsen if it isn't addressed.

These reasons are more than enough to make you understand the value of resolving the anxiety. Your attempts to eliminate the tensions in the relationship show how much you value your relationship. This not only strengthens your bond, but makes the relationship long-standing.

You can develop a healthy relationship by decreasing and eliminating the difficulties. If you are sincere in your effort, your partner will do the same for you and your bond. That is why the little steps and actions make a relationship successful.

No relationship is perfect, and it passes through different phases - but sometimes you hit a bump. What matters is how you tackle the situation; either let it be or try to solve the problem. Always search for the primary disturbance and understand the point of view of your partner. Joint efforts are essential for a long-lasting relationship.

A little bit of effort will save your relationship from falling apart. You can save yourself from a long depression by resolving minor anxiety in your relationship.

This book aims at guiding you to save your relationship by eliminating anxiety and stress in it.

Every partner, for whatever reason, struggles to be perfect at the start. However, you can transform these insecurities into trust and understanding by displaying your love through actions and communication.

The list for saving a relationship and building a healthy relationship is long. We have discussed every possible problem and its solution for having a perfect relationship in this book at great lengths.

A healthy and long-lasting relationship becomes an immense source of joy for a lifetime. So, read and follow this guide if you value your relationship and love your partner.

CHAPTER 1: INTRODUCTION TO RELATIONSHIPS AND ANXIETY IN RELATIONSHIPS

The beauty of a relationship lies in the uniqueness which varies from individual to individual. Each person brings unique characteristics to a relationship. As a result, no two relationships or their requirements are the same.

A relationship is more of an emotional bond with equal responsibility on each partner. When you enter into a relationship, you accept a person with their perks and their flaws.

You need to know your relationship in-depth, just like you know your partner. Determining the type of relationship you're in will save you from a lot of trouble. You can quickly figure out what the problem is if you encounter one. This knowledge will also help build the relationship if you are well-aware of your situation.

The anxiety only emerges when you fail to meet expectations and do not know what the situation demands. Whatever relationship you have, make sure that it is healthy and free of anxiety. Here are the types of relationships there are, so you can figure out what yours is:

Types of Relationships

Codependent Relationships

A codependent relationship occurs when both partners rely on each other to function emotionally, psychologically, or physically. One partner may be more dependent than the other one. Being with each other makes them habitual, and so that they cannot function separately.

It is not wrong to expect and depend on your partner; in fact, missing your partner builds a strong relationship. But as the excess of anything is not good, sometimes codependence exceeds the limits of what makes it healthy. Make certain that your dependence on your partner does not suffocate them and that it does not diminish your individuality.

A codependent relationship is only good until you become repressed, or your partner becomes so. If you have such a relationship, try to maintain the individuality of both of you. Also, cater to each other's needs to avoid tension and stress.

Independent Relationships

An independent relationship is the complete opposite of a codependent relationship. Both the partners do not rely on each other and are not burdened for the other person's needs. Instead, they like to be independent and be themselves while being in a relationship. But the key to maintaining such a relationship is to find the balance and extent of independence. There should be a link and connection that makes you realize that you are in a relationship and have someone special in your life.

When in an independent relationship, you should show interest in each other's lives and build trust while maintaining your unique personality.

Dominant-Submissive Relationships

This kind of relationship develops between two people who are at their extreme negative and opposite sides. One person asserts complete control over the life of another, while the second person gives in to the partner's orders. It is like taking control of one's whole life, and the second person willingly yields to the power of the partner. This relationship is not healthy at all.

This case harms the mental health of the submissive partner as that one is left with no self-confidence. Such a relationship is nothing but emotional torture, and the only way out is to break free or talk your partner out of dominance. If you are being dominant, try to overcome your habit of this and give your partner a fair share of everything. This relationship will only work if there is a sense of self-esteem, which reduces anxiety.

Open Relationships

The open relationship is like an independent relationship, but it does not involve commitment. Both partners are not bound to each other, and they can see anyone they want. This relationship is prone to jealousy and mistrust as it does not involve commitment and security. If you feel anxiety, it is justified. Make it a proper relationship or fall prey to instability, as such a relationship usually does not work for long.

Long-Distance Relationships

A long-distance relationship is unique when partners are at a physical distance. This distance may be as distant as separate countries. A long-distance relationship faces physical barriers more than emotional limitations. If you are in a long-distance relationship, you should communicate continuously to avoid anxiety and distress of any kind.

The Stages of Relationships

The next thing you need to understand about relationships is the stages they go through. These stages are not linear, and sometimes they can happen in a cycle. You and your partner may return to any phase due to setbacks. And that is when your stamina and capability to tackle a relationship crisis are put to the test. You and your partner work things out with mutual understanding while going through a rough patch. A setback does not mean a breakup, but you can start again by taking a few steps back to save the relationship. So, let's find out the stages of a relationship.

Merging Stage

The famous honeymoon phase is this stage, when you are in awe of each other. After a quick and possibly awkward start, you get comfortable with each other, and the honeymoon phase begins. This stage is filled with charm and enthusiasm after getting together. You will feel a rush of feelings for your partner, and the urge to stay together is vital as the intimacy makes you disillusioned about other things.

But setting boundaries here is crucial, as they will form the basis for the future expectations in your relationship. Setting temporary high standards affects the relationship in the following phases because the rationale dictates keeping everything within this limit. So, enjoy this honeymoon phase with excitement, but do not take significant steps and watch your actions. You should be mindful of your partner, too, and be aware of the situation and whether you can go for the long term or not.

The Attachment Stage

The attachment stage is where infatuation begins to turn into love. You feel an attachment towards your partner and welcome them as a part of your life. They resemble a component that is difficult to remove at the moment. However, not all attachments are healthy, and you must strike a balance. Your attachment style shows a lot about your psychology and your past experiences. Choose a healthy attachment pattern if you want to keep your relationship from trouble. The attachment stage is also when the idea of distance causes pain. You become attached and linked to each other in different ways, and this determines the dimension of your future relationship. You need to keep your rational brain by your side to keep things in balance. There are four types of attachments in a relationship, which are:

Secure Attachment

This attachment style does not guarantee that you will not have problems in your relationship. Still, it does indicate that you are secure enough to accept responsibility for your own mistakes and are willing to seek help and support when necessary. With this attachment, you value your self-worth and find it easy to express your emotions. You can maintain emotional balance and look for healthy ways to deal with conflict in your relationship. When your relationship suffers a setback, you are resilient enough to recover.

When you or your partner does not have any emotional baggage from the past, you do not get insecure about each other. This stems from both partners' self-assurance and sense of self-worth, as neither has any emotional baggage or trauma. This type of attachment strengthens and extends the life of the relationship.

Ambivalent Attachment

Individuals with an ambivalent attachment style, also known as "anxious-preoccupied" or "anxious attachment," are overly needy. They are frequently anxious and uncertain, with low self-esteem. They crave emotional intimacy but are concerned that others will reject them. If you have an ambivalent attachment style, you may be self-conscious about being overly clingy. You may be exhausted by fear and anxiety about whether your partner truly loves you, and you may find it difficult to trust or rely on your partner fully. Your sense of self-worth is heavily influenced by how you feel treated in the relationship, and you require constant reassurance and attention from your partner. You may struggle to set boundaries because you perceive space between you and your partner as a threat.

If you or your partner has an anxious attachment style, something is seriously wrong with your relationship. This kind of attachment makes it hard for the relationship to work. You are always dissatisfied because of too little attachment or too much attachment. Your relationship fails to find a middle ground.

Avoidant-Dismissive Attachment

You may find it difficult to tolerate emotional intimacy if you have this attachment style. An avoidant-dismissive attachment style is the polar opposite of an ambivalent attachment style. People with this style try to avoid emotional connection with others, rather than craving intimacy. If you have this type of attachment, it usually means you value your independence and freedom to the point where intimacy in a relationship makes you uncomfortable. You are prone to ignoring your partner's feelings, keeping secrets, having affairs, and even ending relationships to regain your freedom. You may prefer short-term, casual relationships to long-term, intimate ones, or you may seek equally independent partners. Having this personality type usually indicates that you are content to care for yourself and do not believe you require the assistance of others.

An avoidant-dismissive attachment is a relationship deterrence in actuality. This kind of attachment has old unpleasant experiences that make a person afraid of attachment altogether. So, that person tries to avoid being in a relationship. Whenever they feel emotion towards another person, they sabotage it by flinching away. They either distance themselves from their partner by coming off as overly self-oriented, or become fearful and experience intensive mood changes. This attachment is even more harmful if there is a long-term bond. To make things easier, you must work on your issues by stepping outside your comfort zone and communicating clearly.

Disorganized/Disoriented Attachment

Disorganized/disoriented attachment, also known as fearful-avoidant attachment, can result from intense fear, frequently caused by childhood trauma, neglect, or abuse. People who have this type of attachment believe they are unworthy of love. If you have this type of attachment style, you may find relationships difficult to navigate and become insensitive to your partner.

You may have negative behavioral patterns, abuse alcohol or drugs, and be more violent. While you long for the security and safety of a meaningful and intimate relationship, you also believe you are unworthy of love and are afraid of being hurt again.

The Doubt and Denial Stage

The third stage of your relationship is doubt and denial, which is more rational than the previous two stages. You second-guess yourself about the decision you're about to make. This stage will involve awkwardness and doubts towards each other. To make things work in the long run, you must determine the appropriateness of your choice.

Even if you want your partner to be in your life, you may not agree with some of their qualities. But this is the stage that requires the compromise of accepting unwanted characteristics of your partner without causing a conflict.

If you want to save your relationship from anxiety, save it from conflicts. Learn to manage your anger and disappointment so you can be more accepting of your partner.

The Partnership Stage

The partnership stage entails making a final decision to express your undying love for your partner. Now you have been with your partner for a long time and sometimes things get ugly, making you want to contemplate the future. Make sure you choose the right person for you before beginning a partnership. If not, you can end the relationship with clear communication and understanding.

If you think that the person is right for you, choose your role in the relationship and commit to it. You should realize that no match is perfect, and there will always be certain areas that will need both of you to work on them. This stage necessitates each partner to be patient with the other and accept the other's points of view.

If you communicate all your expectations correctly, this stage is fruitful and rewarding. You can enjoy your love without any worries and experience the thrill again. However, making this stage the final one necessitates dealing with new challenges. Try to grow as a couple together and achieve your goals by supporting one another.

Signs of Tensions In The Relationship

Before everything starts to fall apart, there will be signs of warning that your relationship is not going through a good phase. You need to read those signs, which are carefully dropped by your partner. These signs will be mutual or even give you a warning about anxiety in your relationship. When these signs start showing up, you seriously need to do something to resolve the tension. Here are a few signs that will tell you about how anxiety can manifest in your relationship:

Physical Tiredness

When there is stress in your relationship, you feel annoyed and exhausted. You are not able to sleep properly. This exhaustion and sleep deprivation put you in a state of permanent annoyance and keep you away from intimacy of any kind. It is a clear sign of anxiety as it causes cortisol and adrenaline hormones to be released, suppressing the hormones that keep you happy.

Always Angry With Each Other

When you pass through a rough patch or bad days in your relationship, the situation affects both partners equally. Sometimes, they start venting their suffocation at each other, leading to rifts in the bond. Such uncontrolled actions can even worsen the anxiety in a relationship.

Emotional Unavailability

This unavailability is an alarming sign when you do not care for your partner's emotional state and have no urge to console your partner in tough times. This situation rings a bell for getting couple's therapy, when either both partners or just one become emotionally unavailable.

If you cannot support your partner, what is the meaning left in the relationship? Take this sign seriously and go for counseling if you want to keep your bond intact.

Forgetting The Tuning

Anxiety in the relationship causes a surge in stress hormones. These hormones block your capabilities of understanding your partner. You cannot read your partner's emotional state and just keep thinking about your own emotions. This anxiety makes you inexpressive, disconnected, and haywire. You forget how to tune in and bond with your partner.

Constant Dissatisfaction

Nothing can put your mind at ease when you are emotionally, mentally, and physically disturbed. Even if your partner is trying to help your relationship get back on track, it does not satisfy you.

You are constantly on edge, and any familiar, good gesture cannot satisfy you. This stress is harmful to your relationship and sabotages it like nothing else. If you do not address this issue, you will continue to project anxiety and focus on criticism.

Over-Analysis of Relationship

Anxiety can also be caused by attachment issues, which occur when you constantly think about your relationship and partner. Over-analysis of your relationship is a warning sign of an inappropriate relationship or sabotaging behavior.

There may be another reason behind the over-analysis of your relationship, which is when it's the opposite nature of your partner. When you are hypersensitive, and your partner is insensitive, this also leads to overthinking your relationship.

Low Self-Esteem

An unsupportive partner is to blame for low self-esteem. When you are the only one attempting to work out your relationship and your partner is not putting forth any effort, this is a sign of a failing relationship.

Pessimism

When irritability and miscommunication happen in a relationship, both partners become disappointed about the relationship's future. They cannot find the solution because they do not discuss their reasons for the stress. These problems keep on mounting and getting on the nerves of both partners. This situation leads to extreme pessimism where both people feel like there is no use in trying. You look forward to nothing in the distant future or spending time together as it seems useless. The state of pessimism should ring a bell for you. When you feel extremely low and are not trying for a solution, admit your issue and go for couple's therapy.

Attraction Towards Other People

A strong bond keeps both partners occupied with each other so that there is no chance of betrayal or cheating. When two people are happy together, no one seems attractive to them. But this attraction towards your partner diminishes if you have misunderstandings and complaints. Your mind diverts from your partner automatically and seeks another relationship unintentionally – and both partners feel attraction towards other people. This attraction is a sign of detachment stemming from the stress in your relationship. Try to save your relationship when you think your partner is detached from you.

Wanting To Spend More Time On The Phone

The tension in real life makes one want to get distracted by other things. When your relationship is going through a stressful phase, and you and your partner are distant, both of you develop other activities unintentionally. One of the biggest distractions of modern relationships is the phone. When you or your partner want to spend more time on the phone than with each other, it is not healthy for your relationship. Both partners find a way to escape the stressful reality of their relationship.

Whenever you feel that your phone is becoming a distraction to help you to avoid your relationship, take this sign as a warning to mend the relationship.

Overly Critical of Your Partner

Being overly critical of your partner is the most concerning sign of a troubled relationship. You become a critic of your partner, and you start to dislike the things that did not bother you before. And sometimes, your partner also finds your habits troubling, and you often find yourself engaged in an argument.

You perceive only the negative and weak points of your partner. Your partner's solid attributes and qualities do not impress you anymore, but your intention fixates on negative things only. The negativity and criticism are due to the stress in the relationship that does not let you think otherwise.

The constant criticism turns you against each other, leading to distance and irritation.

Whenever you find yourself in such a situation, analyze yourself in an unbiased way, and apologize to your partner if you are wrong. If you find the criticism of your partner unbearable, you can communicate your stance politely. A peaceful talk is the only way to save the relationship from further crisis.

Admittance And Attempts To Resolve Anxiety

Constant tension is a worrying sign if you are constantly disturbed by the distance between you and your partner. Start looking for the signs that indicate the anxiety in your relationship. If all the signs are there, you should do something to prevent any more significant harm. Breakups are not easy, and they leave a terrible imprint on your mind. You should sort out things to save your relationship.

The first step towards a solution is the admittance of the problem. Some couples keep themselves busy and are oblivious that they have troubles in their relationship. They try to avoid facing the confrontational situation that puts both partners through a test.

When you try to resolve the issues, there will be some light shedding on both partners' behaviors and mistakes. So, couples let things be and avoid the main issue. This attitude escalates the tensions even more. The partners should admit the problem first and then try to break the tensions.

Even if your partner is unwilling to realize these tensions, you should attempt to from your behalf. There are situations when the actions of one partner motivate the other partner to reciprocate positively. Thus, your efforts positively influence your relationship, which will strengthen your bond even more.

Attempts To Resolve Anxiety

Here are a few tips that you should follow to relieve the stress in a relationship:

- Try to reinitiate deep and trusted communication.
- Ensure that you maintain your self-esteem even when you tend to your partner.
- Do not suddenly react when you are under the influence of your emotions. As you know, ***"Haste Makes Waste."*** Irrationally acting while emotions are at peak causes immense damage to your relationship.

CHAPTER 2: THE REASONS AND MANIFESTATIONS OF ANXIETY IN A RELATIONSHIP

When you enter a relationship, you have hopes for a future together with an everlasting bond. But sometimes, things go down south in a relationship, and the relationship seems to slip away from your hands. Relationships are a beautiful thing when everything stays on track. You get good laughs, happiness, and memories of togetherness. But nothing seems good anymore when you start having troubles with your partner. Because anxiety prevents you from seeing the bright side, there can be a slew of obvious stressors in a relationship. You need to flag these causes to save the relationship by solving the issues. A few main issues become the trigger point of anxiety in any relationship.

Trust Loss

Trust loss is the most common cause of anxiety in different aspects. The most significant trust deficit kicks in when a partner seems doubtful about the relationship's future. It is because a relationship's feelings and love in a relationship fluctuate back and forth.

In the beginning, when you or your partner confess your feelings for each other, it automatically brings the safety factor. However, after some time has passed and your feelings of love are not validated, anxiety enters your relationship.

The level of anxiety can also vary over time. It increases with less trust and decreases when partners restore faith. A part of the brain, the amygdala, does not register anxiety in a relationship when there is trust.

However, when there is a slight shift in trust and love, this part begins to cause anxiety.

Trust loss can occur in general terms as well. For instance, you don't believe your partner will be faithful to you, or you do not believe you have your partner's support in difficult times. This trust deficit is the biggest destroyer of a relationship.

Vulnerability To Another Person

Feeling vulnerable to other people is the most significant cause of anxiety in a pre-established relationship. The couple starts having issues of competition for love and safety. There is no feeling of security in the relationship or a reciprocation of love. The anxiety kicks in strongly when you feel like you do not have a person to whom you can go for love. The strength that comes from love fades, and your stress is like never before.

This vulnerability of feeling love or attraction for another person is the main reason for tensions in a relationship.

Constant Comparison

The first thing you need to realize when in a relationship is that there is no concept of perfection. You cannot make everything about you or your partner perfect in every aspect. There will be adjustments and compromises, and these slight imperfections are the beauty of a relationship. When you fail to realize this, anxiety enters your relationship.

You see other couples happy and posing perfectly at parties and compare them with your relationship. This attitude is wrong as you do not know the struggles of every couple. Every couple has their problems, but they only show their good side in public. So, comparing your relationship with another is another reason for anxiety. You keep yourself and your partner under constant pressure to meet false expectations.

Lack of Communication

Do you have the impression that your partner is uneasy and distant? If you avoid discussing your confusions and problems with your partner, this can lead to misunderstandings. The communication gap worsens with time, and the distance keeps growing.

This gap causes stress and tensions between both partners. Both of you cannot discuss what bothers you, leading to mistrust. There can be so many problems and misunderstandings due to miscommunication.

A strong couple shares their sorrows and problems just like their happiness. It gives the security to both partners that they have someone upon whom they can lean. But this sense of safety disappears when you do not share your misunderstandings and problems with your partner. It feels like there is no one to back you up. All of this stress happens because of an absence of communication.

Too Many Distractions

Anxiety can stem from the distance between you and your partner. You become distant from your partner when you are involved in other things too much. Your priorities change, and you put unnecessary things above your partner's needs. These distractions can be of different sorts, i.e., mobile phone, gaming, work, or hanging out with friends. All of these things are good if you keep them to a limit. But problems happen when you put so much energy and time into your hobbies and activities. You become devoid of enthusiasm towards your partner because of these distractions. This distance causes anxiety in a relationship, because your partner is in distress due to your negligence. So, you should prioritize your personal life over these distractions if you want to preserve your bond.

Constant Complaining Behavior

If one thing harms your relationship more than any other, it is the habit of complaining to your partner about everything. These complaints make your partner feel like the relationship isn't good enough, and vice versa. Both partners acknowledge that no one, including the relationship, can be perfect. There will be ups and downs, and you should work through your issues.

You should understand your partner too, as complaining about everything will only distance both of you from each other. These complaints can be about anything, including not giving time to personal habits. The key to a successful relationship is being a little bit flexible, and complaints are quite the opposite of this. You put your understanding on the edge when you make unnecessary complaints.

Physical Distance

A healthy relationship is backed up by physical attachment and involvement, just like an emotional one. Physical intimacy makes the relationship strong and keeps the needs of both partners in check. It also shows how much you love each other, and channels this love into physical intimacy.

But when you become overwhelmed with other things and do not give your partner true intimacy, it causes psychological stress too. The physical distance not only affects your partner, but you as well. There will be annoyance and disturbance in your life.

You may find this stress channeled into other problems that subsequently arise in your relationship. The physical distance takes away the psychological assurance of safety.

The Spontaneity Paradox

This paradox of spontaneity stems from a communication block or miscommunication. Usually, couples experience this paradox at the start of a relationship when they are not accustomed to their partner's habits. A spontaneity paradox is a partner's need that you can only fulfill at that moment; for example, your partner needs a hug, but you cannot understand what they need unless it is said. Though these gestures exist in other contexts, the partner craves them in this context.

The failure to understand leads to the idea that you don't understand your partner. And if your partner tells you about the needed hug, it feels like it is not meant as you are only doing it upon request.

The spontaneity paradox can only be solved by knowing about it and understanding your partner and their cues.

Psychological Insecurities

Previous psychological traumas and insecurities can affect a present relationship negatively. People judge their current relationship and partner by the light of their previous ones. They cannot trust again because of those psychological insecurities, which leads to continuous stress.

None of the partners can be happy in such a relationship because there is no mutual trust. It makes the partner over-possessive and insecure because the subconscious says this relationship will deteriorate too.

These insecurities include jealousy, insecurity about love, abandonment issues, and mistrust. If a person cannot find the cause of these issues, any present and future relationship will be at risk.

This fear is not in the control of the partner, because things were left unsolved after a previous bad experience. That is why constant anxiety leads to further psychological pressure in the relationship on both partners. You should take therapies regarding these insecurities, because that is the only way to have a stable relationship without fears and doubts.

Doubting The Feelings of Your Partner

Your mind starts thinking negatively in any aspect when you are under the pressure of anxiety. There is a possible chance of overthinking your partner's responses and questioning any feelings. This doubt stems from the stress that keeps you distant, and neither of you is trying to relieve the tensions.

The uneasy feeling often arises at the start of a relationship when you have not learned about each other's behaviors. But this can cause severe anxiety in a relationship when you doubt your partner's feelings for you.

Feeling The Loss of Charm

After the early honeymoon phase, the things like attachment and passion start to decrease a little. However, the partners cannot accept this, even though they both want to appear normal. Every normal relationship goes through this stage when things become routine, and childishness appears silly. However, both partners may feel that the relationship is losing its luster at times.

This false perception leads to stress, and when not talked out, partners grow apart emotionally. Sometimes, the loss of charm can be due to other reasons like distractions and insecurities. Either way, this thought triggers anxiety because both partners cannot handle the situation maturely.

Victimization

The victimization of a partner comes from the past bad influence of a failed relationship. People feel insecure and think the whole episode of failure will happen again, so they complain to their partner and do not accept their mistake. Even if some misunderstanding happens, you should think rationally and admit the fault as it takes two hands to clap. When a partner is unwilling to take any responsibility and blames the second partner for misunderstandings, it becomes a habit to act like a victim all the time.

The False Expectation of Mind-Reading

The expectation of mind-reading is the most usual mistake any couple makes. You need to understand that no person is a magician, and doesn't know tricks to read the minds of others. Even if you have a long-standing relationship, one can assess their partner's disturbance but cannot guess the reason. There should be trust in order to communicate about actual problems and troubles if you want your partner to support you.

Pinning the hopes on your partner to know the problem without telling them is a wrong expectation. It makes you less expressive and more introverted, causing your partner to lose interest in keeping the relationship. Communicate about the problems and deal with them together.

Not Knowing Low Spots

Every person is susceptible to habitual low times when passion or enthusiasm is lost. The sense of gloom prevails at that time due to previous experiences. Another reason for low spots at a particular time can be any sad incident of the past around that time. Both partners should know about each other's quiet times so they can support each other.

The problem occurs when a partner does not know and tries to understand the habitual lows of the partner, without knowing what's caused it. Your partner seems to lose interest in everything and needs understanding and support from you. The failure to understand these habitual lows leads to the misconception that the partner is selfish and misunderstanding.

Imbalance of Financial Responsibility

Both partners are responsible for catering to the financial needs. Like the emotional and physical responsibilities, the burden of finances lies on both partners equally. When any partner intentionally shirks away from financial obligation, it creates chaos in a relationship.

It overburdens a partner while freeing another from finances, making him come over as a freeloader.

Another reason can be the mismanagement of money. You both run out of savings when you cannot keep your and your partner's spending in check. There are infinite reasons for the mismanagement of money, but the blame lies on both when in a relationship. This monetary problem makes things ugly between both partners.

Careless Attitude

The biggest reason for anxiety in a relationship is the careless attitude of either partner. A relationship requires both partners to care for each other, including through sickness and trouble. When you do not worry about each other, it causes the idea of carelessness. The partner who shows such a careless attitude comes off as selfish. If not resolved, this selfishness and carelessness cause huge misunderstandings, and your relationship will become vulnerable to anxiety.

Manifestation of Anxiety

The reasons we mentioned previously are the leading causes of anxiety in a relationship. Even if there is another issue, you can sense the tension by reading the signs as anxiety manifests itself physically and mentally. You need to know these manifestations of anxiety in order to solve the root cause and save the relationship.

- You find you or your partner are often silent and disinterested in shared interests. Both of you seek assurances excessively on different matters, which imply the underlying insecurity.
- The physical manifestation of anxiety includes sleeplessness, as your troubles do not let you sleep peacefully. You will feel tired due to the distress caused by the deprivation of sleep. The feeling of exhaustion overwhelms you all the time because anxiety triggers the release of hormones for tackling stress.

- There will be tension in your upper body muscles, including neck and shoulder muscles. This tension is a sign of continuous stress in the relationship. Excessive anxiety will cause stress in the back muscles, and you will feel back pain all the time.
- You often find yourself brooding on negativity and finding the reason for anxiety. This overthinking leads to migraines.
- Another significant manifestation of anxiety is sweating despite the weather outside. When tensions escalate in your relationship, stress increases, and your body starts sweating as a response. Excessive sweating happens because of the activation of the sympathetic nervous system, which causes the triggering of sweat glands to release sweat.
- The body becomes short of oxygen when under tremendous amounts of stress, as the body needs blood quickly. You start panting and breathing heavily to catch some air, and it triggers even more anxiety.
- When under a great deal of anxiety, your digestive system gets messed up. You will feel continuous diarrhea, constant stomach pain, and

gastrointestinal distress. These digestive problems occur because stress disturbs the enteric nervous system, which governs the gut-brain axis.

These reasons and manifestations are alarming for your relationship. When these manifestations start showing, you should try to find solutions to the problem of this anxiety affecting your relationship. These physical symptoms show after a long duration of stress when the issues seem out of hand. You should take these manifestations seriously and ask your partner to help you solve these matters.

CHAPTER 3: START BRIDGING THE GAP

Anxiety in relationships is a problem that millions of people face all over the globe. It can cause severe stress in personal and social relationships because a lack of faith causes it. To begin, use good communication skills to bridge the gap.

Begin to close the gap between you and your partner by using comprehension skills, perceiving relief, and treating your anxiety. Don't look at the issue as insignificant. Anxiety is a serious issue that deserves to be treated with respect and compassion. If it were nothing, your partner wouldn't have been so concerned in the first place.

In relationships, anxiety tends to bring out the worst. People's minds are constantly working, continuously asking questions. For example, you are concerned about your relationship and worry that it will end, leading to doubts and uncertainties. You seek answers when you are anxious, but the answers are not always readily available.

Acknowledge that you have an issue initially. An inability to handle anxiety is a disorder that requires medical attention. It will be hard to tackle a problem if you do not recognize that anything is wrong.

Then, tell your partner how you're feeling. If you're having trouble coping or your partner is worried about the relationship, seeking help from a professional specializing in anxiety disorders might be beneficial.

Begin to close the distance between you and your partner. Anxiety arises because you experience more ease when there is some distance between you and others. Try to move toward your partner rather than away from them, and see what happens. This act may seem challenging at first, but it will become easier with practice.

Value and acknowledge your partner's efforts to reach out to you. This gesture will go a long way toward assisting both of you in overcoming unnecessary barriers that often keep partners apart.

Get Closer To Your Partner

The term "bridging the gap" defines the transition from not understanding a person to becoming friends with them. It's a process which takes time to complete.

Emotional responses act as a gas pedal, causing you to act in specific ways. If you're feeling enthusiastic, you could perhaps try to talk to your partner about this. If you're anxious, you may try to prevent them. Your emotions can help you get closer to your relationship goal.

Try To Be Understanding

Most relationships face challenges, but it will be easier to get through them with love as a motivator. You must be sure to notify each other of your missteps, but not of your most personal experiences.

You both have the potential to be selfish or anxious at times. This isn't to say that either one of you is incorrect, but dealing with issues that may occur will require a knowledgeable and comprehending relationship.

Love isn't as crucial as understanding. We should put in a lot of effort to help each other rise and blossom.

Knowledge, interaction, and affection are all qualities that you may want to improve in your relationship. You did not choose to fall in love with this individual, nor did your partner.

People in relationships often stop speaking about important issues that upset them, even if they have been upset by them, in order to avoid a conflict. They are afraid of the negative consequences of those discussions, such as criticism and arguments.

When communication fails then your collaborators will attempt to interact through behavior, which is when the silent therapy starts. People frequently use this strategy to get whatever they want from their partners, such as respect, love, and other types of care.

Conflicts Of Values

When one or both partners have significantly different values, this is a significant cause of dissatisfaction in relationships.

Perhaps one person prefers to live in the city while the other prefers to raise their children in the suburbs. Or maybe one person seeks financial security while the other is willing to take career risks in exchange for a greater sense of happiness or fulfillment. When two individuals want significantly different future lives together, this can be a massive challenge, mainly if they fight about this all the time rather than interacting calmly and trying to find compromises.

You can anticipate some dispute if you're in a relationship with somebody who has various different principles to you. It's difficult to meet your wants and needs when you don't see similar ways of life as your partner. But if you want this to work, you'll have to talk about your distinctions, make compromises, and find a path to happiness with each other.

In a relationship, you can try to be understanding with these steps:

1. First and foremost, begin with your partner. We're all talking about ourselves - it's what we

do - however, that doesn't mean we're paying attention to our partner. Ask about their day, coworkers, and relatives – everything that has disrupted or irritated them during the day.
2. When they speak, you must pay close attention and avoid being distracted by what you are doing or making plans to do that day.
3. Please try to recall everything they said. I know it isn't easy, but just because your partner said something doesn't imply you listened, acknowledged, and memorized it!
4. If you don't understand something, ask them to rephrase it or inform them how something came across to you to help clarify it.
5. Don't give excuses for the old days; instead, stay in the moment with the person who appears to mean so much to you.

Support Your Partner

When you're having a difficult time, the first thing you should do is seek out your partner's support. This isn't always the best option, however. By placing your partner in a challenging position, you may end up doing more harm than good in some situations.

If you're having serious doubts regarding your relationship, attempting to separate things is particularly important. It's critical to know how to avoid trying to cause anxiety in your relationship if you're starting to think about splitting up with your partner or would like to check the potential of being single again.

If you know and understand what your partner says, you may discover that they do not require much assistance from you about certain issues.

It takes a lot of effort to be in a relationship. Things can get complicated, and it can feel like you're under a lot of pressure to complete everything. If your partner indirectly expresses their fears and emotions, you must be knowledgeable and empathetic to them when you're in a relationship.

Even if your partner does things that don't make sense at the time, you must be gentle and supportive. You may feel compelled to solve all your issues independently, but an imbalanced relationship can cause you to feel much more anxious than before.

Partners may express their love for one another in a variety of ways. Perhaps one partner enjoys doing numerous small favors for the other, while another wants the grandest gestures. It's critical not to judge one another based on these differences. Acknowledge your partner for who they are and love them in whichever way usually works for both of you!

Here are a few ways to help your partner while also making them feel supported:

A Better Conversation

When interacting with your partner, be straightforward. When raising concerns or breaking bad news to your partner, you must be honest. Do not believe you can get away with saying barefaced lies or overstating to avoid facing the realities of the situation. Sincerity has always been the best policy with regards to supporting your partner.

Remember To Be Considerate

Be considerate of others and pay attention to what they have to say. Your partner could be thinking about a lot of things. They may communicate their fears and concerns in a veiled manner. If they do this, be patient and don't take it personally; instead, try to understand what they're trying to say, even if it doesn't make sense at first.

Listen Better

Listen closely when your partner starts talking about something which worries them if you want to assist them and avoid unnecessary nervousness. Show them how much you value their input by listening to what they have to say rather than thinking about what you could say after that.

Wait Patiently

For both parties, anxiety can be tiring. It's essential to remember that your partner isn't operating at their greatest when they're anxious. They may require reassurance more frequently than usual, and they may appear clingy and needy. Allow them the time and space to deal with their symptomatology without being judged or criticized. If you're getting annoyed, take a step back and think about things from your partner's point of view.

More Involvement In Each Other's Lives

First and foremost, we should make every effort to become involved in each other's lives. We can boost our participation and workspaces in this way, regardless of the differences.

Start bridging the gap for both you and your partner by keeping in contact with them, learning about their daily activities, and more.

Telling your partner that their job stinks or that you need them to do things differently won't get you more involved in each other's lives. It may make you feel better, but it will not assist you in achieving your goals.

When you can trust people, relationships will always be valuable. The best thing you can do is to start bridging the gap between yourselves.

Tell your partner how passionate you are about them. Talk to them about a variety of topics relating to love and relationships. If both of you are willing to work on it, you can improve your relationship with each other.

Start closing the gap in your relationship by becoming more involved in each other's lives. Each time you do this, you can end up making the bridge a tiny bit broader and more powerful.

For years, many people have already been attempting to make relationships work, but most of them seem to have no idea what they're doing. They don't understand how to accept and love unconditionally. They also know that you're more likely to attract excellent chances when you're happy, but they don't always know how to find that happiness. That's all there is to know about building a great relationship.

With that said, there are a few tricks of the trade that people use in their relationships that you might find helpful if you need to get more involved.

Tip 1: Keep a healthy connection with yourself.

Tip 2: Look after your consciousness and love yourself as much as you love your partner.

Improve Your Relationship By Planning Ahead

Planning things with one another and following through with those plans can help you improve your relationship. This act will help you become more involved in each other's lives because you'll have a dinner date scheduled for that night, which means you'll have something to do. You've devised a strategy and assigned it a deadline. If something comes up that prevents you from carrying out your plan, let your partner know as soon as possible so they don't have to wait.

Creating A Special Bond

When you get innovative and come up with new ideas, making the most of your love life doesn't seem to be a chore. Simple activities such as preparing food together or going for a barbeque can help you create lasting memories. Even if you aren't physically together, make sure you spend some time together as a couple – even if it's long-distance. This time will aid in the formation of that bond and the strengthening of your relationship.

Little Gestures

Little gestures are your significant other's entry point into a joyful connection. Small gestures stifle arguments and assistance. Encourage adoring and loving relationships by bridging the gap between partners and engaging in activities together.

Little gestures were founded on the belief that simple moments of kindness enhance our lives and enable us to live more meaningful and purposeful lives.

It's far better to start closing the gap in connection with a small gesture than to repair it with a master plan.

When you're in a relationship, it's common to recognize the minor details about your partner. You know what mouthwash they use, what cornflakes they prefer, and how frequently they burp.

The point is, you've been sticking around for so long that all the little mannerisms have become second nature to you, and it's easy to overlook that these characteristics which are as fascinating to anyone beyond the relationship as watching paint dry. That's why a small act can go a long way toward making your partner feel valued.

After an incident, attempting to rebuild trust or showing your partner that you love them with a small gesture can be a good conversation starter, regarding how you might move forward.

While this is true in some cases, it may be necessary to address the problem in some cases too. At the same time, if something went wrong that was emotionally damaging or intended to hurt in some way, thoughts and feelings continue to run rampant.

When couples are going through a difficult time, handshakes or cuddling can help keep individuals from becoming too severe and potentially explosive. If someone is upset and their partner is unaware, physical contact is enough to signal that it's time for them both to listen rather than protect themselves.

When do you send a sincere thank-you note, or a message of gratitude, after someone has performed something nice for you? We always want to, but we occasionally forget due to our hectic schedules.

To assist you, here are some suggestions for bridging the gap in your relationship with simple gestures:

Keep The Door Wide Open

This step is a great one, and it's not something that happens much these days—not primarily because of women's issues with men who hold doors open, but also because often these people are in such a rush these days that they don't bother. It is customary for a person to keep a door open for their partner. However, if you're out on an early date with your sweetheart and notice that she has her hands full, move aside and keep the door open for her, and do not forget to smile!

Make The First Move

The old saying "actions speak louder than words" remains steadfast in relationships. If you don't think your partner loves you sufficiently, show them that you can bring benefits. Wash the dishes after an evening meal if your guy is a fantastic cook but despises doing the dishes. It will be a thoughtful gesture that demonstrates your concern for him.

Sending Flowers

There are times in your life that you'll have to deal with the people you dislike for various reasons. Although you do not like an individual, the smartest thing you could do in this scenario is to find a way to become much more friendly with them. Bring flowers to begin bridging the relationship's gap. It might be a good idea to change the person's mind to see things from your point of view. Flowers are an excellent place to begin, since almost everyone recognizes them as a kind gesture. You might like to think about some of the reasons why it might be beneficial to send flowers when trying to make friends with someone.

Creative Gift Ideas

Use your imagination when it comes to gift-giving. It's a time to rejoice and be surprised. So, don't limit yourself to chocolates or jewelry. Instead, give something that will aid in the development of your relationship. Give a framed photo of the two of you or a certificate for a special occasion, such as a weekend getaway or food preparation class – something which you can do together.

Surprise Your Partner With A Memory Book

Giving your partner a vacation surprise is a fantastic way to reignite the fire in your relationship that once burned brightly. Try to amaze your partner with older pictures of the two of you, as well as gifts you believe they will appreciate. Don't be astonished if your partner begins speaking about memories and reminisces about the great times you two shared when you were still dating. If this occurs, you can rest assured that your surprise was successful!

CHAPTER 4: DO NOT SMOTHER EACH OTHER

In a relationship, don't suffocate each other. One of the most common blunders is strangling your partner by being overly controlling and emotionally needy. If they leave after spending time with you, don't think it counts against them. Keep the flame of love burning. When you're on your way to a relationship, be cautious.

Your happier half should never be the source of your joy. If this happens to a relationship, it's time to get it back on course. Lovebirds frequently get away with their actions because they are motivated by love. Smothering without permission, on the other hand, is unethical. Relationships require interaction, belief, sincerity, and common ground.

Every relationship reaches a breaking point at some point. It could be a situation involving smothering or another issue. It could be the start of a massive storm that will cause a great deal of stress and disruption.

When you're in a relationship, you're both willing to take responsibility for each other. Please don't make your partner feel like you are strangling him. Allow him to breathe and avoid being too emotionally needy. Start giving more than you take from him; making major concessions will support him.

You must be prepared for the possibility that the person you love will not be the same person in twenty years' time.

A person's life can undergo a series of differences, especially after getting married. It's okay if the person changes to better the two of you.

Allow distance in your relationship so that instead of bothering each other, you can both take a breath. Several people have control issues and believe they have complete control over their partner's lives, allowing them to do whatever they want without being dominated or interfered with. This mindset will only lead to strife between two lovers.

When you try too hard to make your significant other happy, you may end up making them uncomfortable in the relationship. This suffocation is due to your lack of respect for your partner's autonomy.

Try to strike a balance among both, keeping them laughing and enabling them to be self-sufficient Even if your partner's choices do not bring you happiness, you must respect them. You will not have authority about how they handle you, but you do possess power about how you respond to it!

Suppose your boyfriend or girlfriend is spending more time with friends and family than they were before you even began dating. In that case, it's a positive indication that they're moving closer to independence. On the other hand, if they constantly monitor you and request where you have been at all hours of the day, they do not honor your autonomy.

Too Much Closeness Has A Negative Impact

If you're in a relationship, you're most likely to speak regularly and spend time with your partner. However, experts contend that too much affection is terrible for a relationship and that the ideal level of love is just how close the couple is.

Don't strangle your relationship with love. You'll only irritate each other and push one another away. Keep a safe distance from one another to avoid driving each other insane. It's critical to keep a certain amount of space from your partner in a relationship.

When you become too emotionally intimate with someone, it can hurt your relationship. You must be willing to share your partnership with others for your relationship to develop. Even the most satisfying, long-term relationships require some breathing space now and then.

There's a thin line between caring for your partner and suffocating them. It can be challenging to know how to care for someone without going too far.

Here are a few ways that being too close in a connection can harm you as well as your partner:

Emotionally Abusive Relationship

In an emotionally abusive relationship, you feel as if you're being suffocated. You want the other individual to be around for love and support in a happy relationship. An emotionally abusive relationship can feel disturbing, as though you're starting to lose yourself when your partner is constantly present or gives useless advice or criticism. You may find yourself attempting to avoid your partner or losing your temper with him for no apparent cause.

Losing Yourself In A Relationship

When you lose yourself in a relationship, your identity is taken away from you. A relationship should improve your quality of life rather than take it over. It's unhealthy if your partner has such control over your life that you don't have time for yourself. You risk losing your sense of self and becoming reliant on your partner for everything from enjoyment to joy. You've grown tired of each other. Once you understand each other that well, boredom and frustration can develop. When this occurs in a romantic relationship, it may result in cheating or divorce.

Isolating Your Partner

Isolating your partner from the rest of the world is unhealthy. It's an early indicator that the relationship is one-sided. If you need proof, try encouraging your partner to spend time with other people without you and see how the relationship improves.

Controlling Partner

Another sign of unhealthy closeness is attempting to control your partner. Excessively controlling behavior can quickly drive your partner away. Furthermore, it is a sign of your poor self-esteem and feelings of inadequacy. The top focus should be togetherness and respect for one another's freedom, rather than attempting to control or manipulate events.

Being Too Reliant

Being overly reliant on a partner can hurt a relationship. Being reliant tends to make you needy and helpless while making the other person feel trapped and feel shame at the same time. Since it inhibits you from acquiring new skills, this reliance can prevent you from being effectively active and independent.

Giving Space

If you don't need to be together all the time in a relationship, start allowing the other person some space for themselves, and you'll have more room for yourself. That is why you must identify and characterize the factors in the relationship before sticking to them.

When you share a place with another person, it's natural for things to feel a little cramped. To stay happy in a relationship, give each other space.

Allow your relationship to grow and breathe while remaining close enough to spend quality time together and fall passionately in love again.

When you're in a new relationship, it's tempting to stick to your schedule and hang out with your partner all the time, but resist this urge. To keep your love alive, you must give each other some distance. It's also crucial to avoid suffocating one another.

Any pair who have been together more than just a few months should make plans for a few "date nights" in the coming week. They don't have to be elaborate outings; all you need is some time away from work or family to enjoy each other's company. Simultaneously, don't spend too much time with each other.

Even if you enjoy being near one another all of the time, it can help you feel as if everything is too comfortable and that they are taking your relationship for granted. Even a seemingly happy person may become dissatisfied in the long run due to this. Too much time together can lead to taking one another for granted. It's perfectly acceptable to set aside some time for yourself and your friends.

How to give your partner the appropriate amount of space:

Allow Each Other To Be Alone

You mustn't always go out with each other, constantly text each other, or spend too much time around each other. Alone time can sometimes bring people closer together. Allow your partner to pursue their own interests without having to feel neglected or lonely.

Spend Some Time Apart From Each Other

In many partnerships, just like in many relationships, there must be "we" and "me" time. Allow each other to spend time with family and friends without feeling obligated to each other, and pursue your own goals without feeling obligated. Examine whether someone is consistently going above and beyond for someone else without receiving anything in return. Taking a pause will help you maintain control and avoid feelings of dissatisfaction or frustration.

Respect Their Privacy

In most relationships, both partners can have their own private space. The right to privacy must be respected. Intruding too deeply into someone's personal life can make them feel uncomfortable. By not calling or texting each other frequently, you respect each other's privacy. Couples must respect each other's privacy to be happy and healthy.

You must keep some parts of your life private if you want to have a healthy relationship. That's all there is to it.

If you want to be in a serious relationship, you must respect your partner's private information. You might not realize it at first, but once you do, you'll recognize the value of privacy in relationships and how it might strengthen the bond between the two of you.

Respect is essential. You're on your path to a better relationship when you respect each other's privacy and independence.

Many couples are unaware of what they can do to protect their privacy, which can have severe consequences once a relationship has ended.

The amount of privacy required by each couple varies. On the other hand, more liberty will make you feel at ease with one another, whereas more limitations will strain your connection. Above everything, keep yourselves from suffocating each other by honoring one another's privacy.

In a relationship, maintaining privacy can be difficult. We all have a side of ourselves that we don't want anyone else to see, but when you're with someone who means more than a casual fling, you want to tell your partner everything.

It's a delicate balancing act to strike the correct balance between respecting your partner's confidentiality and their need for affection. Most couples manage to strike the right balance without incident. Still, if you believe your relationship is suffering from something you do not want to share that requires being said, it's time to have an open and honest discussion.

If you want to keep a healthy connection, respect each other's privacy. Personal discussions, private emails, and third-party contact information are the three types of personal data you must keep secret in your connection. Here are some ideas for how to respect each other's privacy in a relationship:

Private Discussions

Don't discuss your partner's intimate matters with others, even if they are your friends. Such discussions will crush their hearts and may cause your connection to deteriorate. Instead, have an open and honest conversation with your partner in private.

Private Emails

Don't try to decipher or skim through your partner's emails or texts. You don't have such a privilege. Leave them alone; if you are wary of them, it is sometimes none of your business! You need them to feel safe in your company.

Contacts with Third Parties

Please don't contact your partner through other people, such as relatives, friends, work colleagues, or exes, unless they specifically asked you to do so. Don't contact them through a third party if they do not want you to.

Under no circumstances should you interact with them unless they specifically request it.

A Little Emotional Independence

There will always be a sense of reliance between lovers and married people in everyday life. The more adoration you have for your partner, the more essential it is for you to develop complete emotional independence.

Allow one another emotional independence - from the other person's perspective and from how you're used to it, and you can also prepare for a joyful couple's life around each other.

Start loving one another, and you will feel empowered; a spirit of common ground is advantageous to any relationship. Emotional independence, particularly in relationships, is the way to happiness. You must strike a balance between reliance and personal autonomy, just as you must in life. You don't have to expect everything from your partner just because you're in love.

Many people will try to suffocate each other if they have some emotional independence. Before they can even honestly and sincerely love another person, people have to love themselves initially. You won't be capable of giving love to anybody if you don't love yourself first. You must accept that there will always be people who will hurt you; however, you will not allow them to hurt you if you love yourself. Allow your partner to breathe and be there for them if they need you.

The best thing that could happen in a relationship is if you're two separate individuals. That way, if your partner does anything crazy, you won't have to change who you are as a result. Furthermore, if your partner does something stupid, you can feel free to enlighten them about that without fear of compromising the relationship.

Understanding the difference between independence and freedom is critical for both partners. Many people believe that being in a relationship entails giving up all of one's freedom, but this is not true. When you're with someone you care about and trust, you should feel free and more open, not less so.

So, here are a few pointers to help you gain some emotional independence:

- Expect your partner to respond differently every time; they can express themselves how they want.

- You may be yelling at them for not returning your calls or messages, but keep in mind that it is their life, and they will determine how and when to react.
- Nobody and nothing in this globe, including your partner, is under your regulation. Till the end of time, you will not be able to do this. However, you can impact someone by being there for them, but you'll never influence them by trying to force guilt or frustration on them.

Attempting to take over the minds of others is a surefire way to destroy relationships. Treating others as equals is the best way to avoid this. You'll notice that their capacity to be self-sufficient improves due to this. They may not agree with everything that you do or say, but they will recognize the fact that you are free to make your own decisions rather than attempting to control them.

Trying it out for yourself is a great way to know emotional independence. See what occurs when you quit trying to make other individuals make choices for you, and instead begin making your own choices. You might be pleasantly surprised at how it worked out!

CHAPTER 5: RELATIONSHIP COUNSELING

When things seem to go out of hand and there is no way out of the endless problems, your number one option is relationship counseling. Relationship counseling is seeking the help of experts who can solve the dilemmas and issues you are having as a couple. Counseling creates a safe space for you and your partner to share your deep-down feelings. You and your partner become comfortable in sharing your fears and troubles. Both of you leave matters in the hands of the counselor, but relationship counseling is just a means to help you share and sort out your problems. You are both working on your issues, and a counselor acts as a catalyst to this process.

But first, both of you must recognize that you have difficulties that you cannot fix on your own. It would be beneficial if you just went to relationship therapy when you were both on the same page about doing so. Otherwise, it will appear to be pressuring your partner into doing something they don't want to do.

There are specific therapies that you can do on your own before going to a counselor. Let us dig into the self-therapy you can do as a couple to save your relationship.

Self-Therapy

Finding The Point When Problems Began

The key to solving any problem is finding when and where the crisis began. You need to trail back to the roots of the problem to find the point from which it is emerging. The main point of confusion and trouble needs to be solved. Otherwise, it will be like shooting arrows in the air. The root cause can be minor or significant, but it will become the basis for further problems. And you will notice things getting worse after a particular issue or trouble.

You can solve the problem, talk it out, make gestures to show the importance of your partner in your life, and even translate your insecurities. The problem may lie in your past relationships and fears stemming from them. The problems start when you channel negative energy from your past and future worries. That is often the leading cause of anxiety in relationships.

Another problem could be the lack of understanding or the creation of misunderstanding. There could be many reasons that worsen with time, due to a lack of good communication. That is why pinpointing the root of the problem is essential.

Anxiety in a relationship can be due to the uncertainty about the future, which makes both partners anxious. It would help if you found out when and why that uncertainty began and what led to this uncertainty. Human nature fears uncertainty as they do not know what is coming for them. The human mind creates myths and misunderstandings to cope with overthinking. This overthinking and tension cause emotional chaos; that is why you need to find out what is causing this uncertainty and when it entered your relationship.

You can sit down alone or with your partner to find the source of the problem. Both of you should strive to save your relationship, as you have an equal share in a relationship. And the first thing you need to do before finding the solution to a problem is work on the acceptance of that problem.

Giving Up The Ego And Forgetting The Past

Couples sometimes drift apart due to the towering egos that do not let them try to save the relationship. This ego is the enemy of a healthy relationship, and it is not equivalent to self-esteem that people perceive wrongly. There will always be some bumps and problems in a relationship. But a healthy relationship should have understanding and the ability to look past the egos.

You should know that no one is perfect, and both of you are vulnerable to making mistakes. But both of you should have the audacity to tackle these problems without letting your ego interfere and mess up the relationship. You and your partner should keep your egos aside to resolve the issues. When you know what is causing the anxiety in a relationship, your first thought should be, "Let's solve this." But sometimes, the ego stops you from talking to your partner as you fear that you may come off as trying too hard. This thought is purely egoistical and harms your relationship, as you get a positive response only when you take a positive step. You need to solve the relationship with your partner's involvement, keeping your ego aside and resolving the anxiety.

The second thing which is important for saving a relationship is forgetting the past. Whoever committed the mistake should accept and apologize and move past these negativities. It will do you no good to keep reiterating your partner's history and mistake-shaming. Your partner will not feel secure and trusted anymore. The anxiety will prevail in your relationship because of remembering past mistakes.

Forgiveness of The Mistakes

The traditional dynamics of a relationship have become obsolete. This change is because of the digitalization of our worlds, leading to less intimacy and involvement in each other's lives. The partners often hide behind the false comfort of their screens, ignoring each other and the problems in their relationship. This situation worsens the already-present anxiety in the relationship. But it would help if you showed more involvement in each other's lives as soon as you figured out the root cause of the problem. And most of the problem is due to less intimacy, more digitization, and ignoring the problem.

But you can save the relationship when you move past these trivial obstacles. Try to solve the problems and forgive each other for their mistakes in the past. Forgiveness is key to saving a relationship and strengthening the bond. When you are in the process of forgiving, your mind is more receptive to positive energy. Both of you look at your mistakes, admit them, and move past the obstacles which are causing anxiety in your relationship.

Working On Weak Areas

There are always highs and lows in a relationship, along with emotional insecurities. When evaluating your behaviors and trying to solve the relationship, you should work on these weak areas that cause anxiety in your relationship. You should figure out which weak points of you and your partner are misunderstood by you both.

Sometimes one of the weak areas is the emotional intensity, which causes disturbances and fights. You both need to find whose emotional intensity and tendency to act up is causing harm to your relationship. These weak areas cause anxiety in your relationship when left unsorted, because problems will keep repeating themselves.

You need to talk to each other and ponder how to solve your weak points. Otherwise, these problems will become irritated nerves that will keep hurting you whenever you act up. Figure out what these weak points are and what the reasons behind them are. You can work on these areas individually or together as well. But solving this issue using both individual and together approaches will bring more strength and solutions to your relationship. You will find ways of working out your problems, which will lead to the long-term strengthening of your relationship.

Professional Relationship Counseling

You can solve many problems by self-counseling and attempts on your own, but if you feel like the anxiety in the relationship is kicking in again, it is time to seek professional counseling. Professional counselors extend help to couples who have been on the verge of breaking up despite not wanting to get separated because of unresolved issues. These counselors have the expertise to stabilize your relationship and alleviate the anxiety you face as a couple.

There is no shame in reaching out to a couple of counselors. This step shows how much you are putting effort into saving the relationship. The relationship counselor not only resolves your conflicts, but tries to spark up the love you had.

History of Relationship Counseling

Relationship counseling dates back to the 1920s, but modern couples' therapy started in 1940-1950 in the United States. Many famous eugenics promoted couples counseling, including Paul Popenoe, Robert Latour Dickinson, and Hannah Stone. But the proper counseling began in the late twentieth century, when psychologists started counseling couples for their problems. Before that, the counseling only focused on couples facing severe psychological issues. But nowadays, good marriages and couples' counselors help teams save their relationships.

How Couples Counseling Saves A Relationship

A relationship counselor can save your relationship from further anxiety and give you valuable insight into the relationship. There will be conflicts due to differences, and the counselor helps you both if they exceed your problem-solving capacities.

The counselor will provide you with techniques with which to navigate the challenges of a relationship and show you ways to make your bond strong. These techniques will keep helping you, even if you are done with the therapy in the long run. Here are a few aspects through which therapy saves your relationship:

Improved Communication

The base of deterioration of a relationship is poor communication or a lack of communication from both partners. The couples' therapy makes you sit together and communicate all the problems, so you can deal with them rationally. You learn to communicate to resolve the anxiety in the short-term, and long-term communication to keep anxiety from happening again.

Closeness

Relationship therapy saves your marriage or relationship by triggering the urge to become close again. The anxiety causes the loss of intimacy first. You become close again by solving all the issues acting as barriers and keeping you distant. Closeness is the prime need for keeping the relationship intact, and therapy works on this as a priority.

Trust Building

Anxiety causes distrust between both partners due to misunderstandings and conflicts. This anxiety happens because of the loss of trust in the first place, as both partners think they have become estranged. If you want this trust to build again, you should go for counseling. The counseling will make you sit together and build trust by expressing your true selves and thoughts.

Setting Boundaries

When both partners cross the set boundaries and invade private space, it causes trouble. The violation of boundaries causes anxiety, and therapy makes both of you realize the importance of this issue. A counselor points out which boundaries you need to set to keep your relationship together. Your relationship needs to be saved when you cannot set your limits, and a counselor plays the role of savior by setting boundaries.

Resolving Disputes

Disputes are usually the main reason you need counseling as a couple in the first place. Disputes triggered by various reasons are not easily solvable. A counselor works on finding the history of a particular dispute and the reasons that caused it. You should be honest with your counselor if you want to save the relationship.

The counselor acts as a mediator, to negotiate the conflicts that you cannot solve independently

Recognizing The Pattern

When your relationship starts to face anxiety, there will be patterns of triggers and disturbances. You cannot find or identify these patterns on your own because of the distress surrounding them. But a counselor is an expert at finding the root cause of a problem. You report all your behaviors and problems to your counselor in order to identify the patterns of anxiety and how it gets triggered.

Steps To Saving A Relationship by Professional Counseling

A relationship counselor performs the therapy in eight steps, with your involvement. Following these steps is necessary to resolve all your conflicts and strengthen the relationship. Here are the steps that couples have to undergo during relationship therapy:

Step 1: Professional relationship counselors give you a specific time frame to observe your behaviors when you go to professional relationship counselors. You have to find out which things cause misunderstandings and conflicts during that particular time; let it be a week or so. Your counselor gets an overview of your triggering areas and then designs the counseling program for you both. The triggers are rooted in problematic behaviors for coping with the past, or simply embedded in your schema.

Step 2: When your counselor figures out what schema or behavior is causing conflict between you and your partner, you have to deal with these things. There might be a chance that you both get triggered during your counseling session, but this trigger is needed for you to face your weak points.

Step 3: This step involves working on your avoidance strategies. You and your counselor find values and different approaches to save the relationship. These approaches are necessary for dealing with the schema pain and behaviors. This step is about letting you choose between saving your relationship or keeping your pain hidden. You need to face your pain and choose your response to deal with it.

Step 4: This step involves discussing the topic that is causing conflict. Your anxiety in a relationship worsens because you avoid facing your fears. The counselor makes you observe your problematic behavior by opening the discussion on emotional pain.

Step 5: This step is about observing the problem more than solving the problem. You have to note down the particular time, the reason, and the signs of triggering behavior. There will be signs like a change in voice tone, facial expression, posture, and hand gestures. These signs are the cues you use while avoiding the issue.

Step 6: The counselor encourages you to face your avoidant behaviors during this step. You both come face to face to describe your feelings out loud. The counselor asks you to communicate pain, needs, and emotions right at that moment when you are vulnerable.

You have to convey your feelings honestly but keep your tone mild in order to portray your intentions sincerely and carefully. The counselor asks you what you are feeling while expressing these emotions, and you have to focus on what matters in your mind right now. Keep physical touch like holding hands, touching, or eye contact while communicating your feelings.

Step 7: You must work on problem-solving based on core values. Start with validating the pain you both are experiencing and admit it as the barrier between you and your partner. Now, start to solve your problem by creating gentle communication.

You and your partner should take turns to propose solutions to the conflict and address the needs that are not getting fulfilled. The therapist cheers you and facilitates the process by encouraging you and acting as a catalyst to the problem-solving method.

Step 8: Your therapist makes it easier for you to take responsibility and notice the moment of the avoidance. This step makes you responsible and mindful of your relationship. You have to sit together, resolve the issue, and remind yourself how much you both value your relationship.

CHAPTER 6: UNDERSTANDING THE IMPORTANCE OF COMMUNICATION

Your relationship's durability depends on your ability to communicate with your partner. When a pair is in love, it's rare that they don't fantasize about fairy tales and are always eager to show compassion.

Communication, however, disintegrates with the flow of time and the stresses of the daily struggle.

Examining the importance of interaction when handling conflict is essential for better communication and good relationships. Effectively managing disputes and interactions lays the foundation for genuine relationships and affection.

The lifeblood of any connection is communication. This is the best way to hear each other's thoughts and emotions.

Meeting in person or through social media is the most critical aspect of any relationship. It can be simple or complex, short and simple, or lengthy and elaborate.

A good relationship requires open communication. It helps to express your emotions and thoughts to your partner while also assisting you in understanding theirs. It makes you feel more connected to one another.

When one or both partners in a connection fail to express themselves, problems arise. This issue can lead to miscommunications and disagreements.

Any relationship relies heavily on communication. When a couple is fighting, it could be challenging to figure out what's wrong and how to fix it. If a couple has very little interaction, they may well not realize

ANXIETY IN RELATIONSHIP

they are wandering off from each other and that this could lead to future troubles.

A couple should first acknowledge the importance of good communication and why it is required, before learning how to communicate successfully with each other. It's also beneficial to understand what constitutes excellent communication and improve communication skills.

Here are some suggestions for improving communication:

- Make it a point to spend some quality time with one another regularly. To tell your partner about your day might very well make you develop closeness.
- Discuss any issues bothering you as quickly as possible so they don't grow over time and later blow up into an argument.
- Even if it's humiliating or ends up hurting somebody else's emotions, start sharing what's troubling you instead of keeping it to yourself. Trying to keep things bottled up inside will only cause you to feel much worse, and will cause long-term troubles with your partner.
- So that you do not lose contact with what is taking place and start creating excuse after excuse

for everything, be truthful with yourself and your partner.

- Allowing conflicts to fester will only lead to more considerable trouble down the road. Instead, try working over them as a group as early as possible before they grow into something more serious.

What Is Proper Communication In A Relationship?

The importance of communication in a relationship cannot be overstated. There would be so many issues in a relationship if interaction were not present. There can be no comprehension, adoration, or respect if there is no understanding.

In a relationship, interaction is the process of sending and receiving details. It can also be classified as a non-verbal process in which people use words, facial gestures, and other body language to convey themselves, share experiences, and exchange thoughts, emotions, and concepts.

Partners establish confidence, develop relationships, and resolve issues through communicating effectively.

It helps us understand that communication is essential by looking at the different types of conversations. Face-to-face and non-verbal communication are the two main types.

It can be hard to communicate with somebody you live with regularly. It takes a lot of planning and hard work for most couples to ensure that their discussions are efficient and valuable.

To communicate effectively in love, both partners must listen actively to and respond to just about everything the other one has to say. For the interaction to occur, one must be ready to listen and speak their mind when necessary. Communication skills are beneficial in all relationships, but they are essential in love relationships in which both parties share emotions, opinions, and desires.

Verbal and non-verbal are the two types of communication:

Verbal Communication

When you speak or read with your voice, you use verbal communication. Verbal communication can be beneficial when working together to solve problems or make decisions.

Non-Verbal Communication

Because it includes motions, facial gestures, and body movement, non-verbal communication is also known as body language. You can use non-verbal communication to figure out what the other person is thinking or feeling. This type of communication helps determine someone's position in a situation.

Clean Communication

The Art of Clean Interaction is cutting-edge guidance to effective couple communication. Along with a top relationship expert, you'll learn to cultivate the clarification, boldness, and kindness necessary for a genuine emotional bond.

- In a relationship, be accessible, genuine, and supportive.
- In a relationship, communication is essential. You can make it easier to communicate uncertainty and distance by having clear, frequent, and honest conversations with your partner. Many of us believe we communicate effectively with our partners, but we frequently assume they are aware of our thoughts and feelings.

Any relationship relies on effective communication. You and your partner will need to talk about a lot of stuff; from differences of opinion to romance. On the other hand, your relationship may be jeopardized if you have the bad tendency to fail to communicate or argue.

The great news is that you can interact with and fix your issues with your partner in a healthy way. Here are some suggestions for doing so:

Express Empathy to Your Partner

Actions speak louder than words. If your partner begins to believe that you no longer worry about them, they will feel more safe in the understanding that you have heard and understood and considered their emotions.

By summarizing what your partner has said, you can demonstrate that you were paying attention. This form of communication indicates that you care about your partner's thoughts and feelings, enabling them to understand that you value their thoughts and feelings and thus value them.

Be Respectful Of Your Partner

No matter what you've been talking about, respect your partner's feelings. Remember that they are human beings with feelings and thoughts, so treat them respectfully.

Don't Get Angry

Try not to get mad or protective when interacting with your partner or discussing touchy subjects. When you disagree with something they say, it's easy to lose your cool, but staying calm and composed will enable you both to work through the scenario more effectively.

Be Truthful

This should go without saying, but it's worth mentioning. In any connection, sincerity is crucial, but it's especially vital when discussing sensitive topics or solving troubles with your partner. Your partner deserves to know the truth from you on all occasions.

Jumping To Conclusions

If at all possible, avoid making assumptions. To save time, avoid forming assumptions about what someone else intends or wants based on the words they've used or the actions they've chosen. You can end up being utterly wrong, which could damage your relationship. If you're unclear about something, ask them, instead of guessing or thinking you know what they're saying.

Commandments Of Communication

Communication is the glue that holds a relationship together. Because men and women are so dissimilar, it's no surprise that communication between them is difficult.

Commitment is a delicate balancing act of discipline and self-determination. Both partners must train in their communication as efficiently as possible (not against each other).

While telling your partner what you need and want is essential to ensuring a healthy relationship, concentrating much more on their requirements than yours can cause your relationship to suffer. So, because once you start to pick apart your partner's behavior and attempt to "fix" them, make sure you're familiar with these six relationship communication commandments:

1. Never say never: If you say you'll never do stuff, your partner will make sure you do it sooner or later.
2. Never go to bed mad: Before heading to bed, help solve any problems, because unanswered

questions cause a lot of sentimental static throughout the night.
3. Never argue in public: When you argue loudly, everyone can hear you and often misinterprets what you're saying.
4. Never make excuses; simply apologize: If you've done something terrible, confess it, apologize, and don't give excuses for your actions, because justifications are just empty words.
5. Never accuse your partner of cheating: If you have concerns about your partner's loyalty, ask them about these concerns rather than jumping to any conclusions and accusing them of trying to cheat on you, since it makes you appear unsafe and insane.
6. Don't ever say you're sorry unless you mean it: An admission of guilt should be sincere, or it should not be made at all; saying "sorry" when you don't mean it is still a lie, and it will erode trust in your long-term relationship.

Communication Problems

Communication issues are the most common causes of relationship problems. Interaction is crucial to the success of any relationship if it's how you communicate with your partner, or how much your partner shares with you.

It's normal for a relationship to have some communication issues. Unless, on the other hand, you discover yourself in more than one argument per week, and your relationship is suffering. As a result, you should start figuring out why you are fighting so much in the first place.

Lack of communication is the most common issue in relationships. If this becomes a problem in your relationship, it may be time to change. Try discussing the case with your partner to see whether they open up more. When all hope is not lost, try going on a trip with each other or doing something particularly unique for the two of you from when you first started dating. This effort could rekindle some good interactions among you two and even strengthen your bond.

If you're having difficulty communicating with your partner, it doesn't mean you'll never be able to find happiness together again. It does, however, imply that you must take action for things to return to normal between the two of you.

Sit down with your partner as quickly as possible and discuss what's affecting the communication issues. You must be upfront and honest with each other about your thoughts and emotions. It may appear to be an awkward conversation at first, but it's critical to keep communicating until you've both had your say.

The next step is to figure out any problem during your presentation. When dealing with a problem with your partner, remember that communication is crucial. If one of you is prone to becoming enraged quickly, it will be more difficult for the two of you to come up with answers to the challenges that arise. Respect one another, listen intently, ask questions, and don't disturb one another when discussing what's troubling you. The following are examples of relationship communication issues:

Failure To Listen Or Ineffective Listening

Once one or both partners refuse to listen to what the other is saying, this problem arises. Worse, one or both partners fail to listen actively, resulting in them misinterpreting what the other partner is attempting to say. You may believe you can predict what your partner will say before they say it, so you end up deciding not to hear. It can be risky because your presumptions about what your partner will say are often incorrect, causing hurt feelings. Sometimes even if you do not intend for this to occur, it may.

A Lack Of Deference

In a marriage relationship, respect is essential because your connection will struggle without it. Care entails appreciating your partner's feelings and views. Without this respect, a relationship can quickly devolve into mutual disrespect and contempt. A lack of respect can result in a communication breakdown, which can be disastrous for a relationship.

Listening To Your Partner In A Relationship

Interaction is among the most crucial components of any happy relationship. The potential to express effective communication between two or more individuals is present. Speaking, listening, reading, writing, and nonverbal communication are all part of it.

It isn't always easy to listen to your partner in a relationship. It can be challenging when you're tired, disturbed, or concerned about other stuff. It's possible that your partner is not putting as much effort into hearing you as you do, which can be aggravating and hurtful.

In a relationship, listening to your partner is a gesture of respect and recognition. It's also the basis of an optimistic connection, which is essential to having a happy relationship.

TIP: If you want your partner to pay attention to you, make very sure you're paying as much attention to them too.

Many people make the mistake of confusing the two. You may have heard your partner's words, but that does not mean you have paid attention to them. You probably hear whatever they are trying to say and have a great understanding of the information when you're genuinely listening.

Rather than thinking about what you want to say next when somebody is speaking to you, concentrate on whatever they are simply stating. If needed, ask questions for clarification. Unless someone asks for advice, fight the temptation to give it. When you're in a relationship, it's easy to forget that your partner doesn't require your guidance.

Be A Good Listener

Listening carefully to your partner is critical in a relationship; this means not jumping into what you would like to say after that, but instead attempting to understand what your partner is telling you. It would be best to make some effort to make your partner feel more comfortable enough to confide in you about their problems and concerns.

Pay Attention

When your partner is speaking, pay attention to what they say; don't try to juggle thoughts while they're informing you of something crucial. You should pay close attention to him and make him feel at ease while speaking.

Giving Your Partner Space To Speak

Try not to disturb or interrupt when your partner provides you with their viewpoint or simply shares things essential to them. When your partner decides to discuss something with you, they will wait for a reply from you. It doesn't indicate that you have to cooperate with them, and you can describe why you don't want to, but try not to be narrow-minded as it can result in conflicts.

Listening

You've probably heard a lot about active listening or paying attention to what somebody is saying. In any relationship, active listening is a critical tool for healing rifts, comforting hurting hearts, and creating an environment where trust and understanding can flourish. "Active" indicates that you are not only listening to what was said, but also displaying that you were listening by repeating back to your partner anything you heard them mention. The following is how it works:

- Rather than considering what you're going to say next after your partner starts talking, pay attention to what they're saying. Pay close attention to their words and tone, and determine whether he appears happy, sad, or mad.
- Be conscious of their gestures, as well as their body language. How could you understand whatever your partner is trying to say if you're wondering what to say after that?
- Reiterate as many of the essential aspects as you can after he's finished talking. First, outline the critical point of the discussion. Then go over some of the key issues brought up during the debate.

Being as precise as possible is the best way to ensure that your overview is accurate.

History

Carl Rogers created active listening as a technique for psychotherapy clients in 1951. The method's goal is to establish a framework for dialogical interaction, in which two or more parties listen to one another to comprehend one another and reach mutual goals. It is a valuable skill that may be applied in various circumstances, including sales, counseling, and negotiations.

Carl Rogers' work on non-directive therapy inspired active listening. Rogers's "non directiveness" theory stressed the need for therapists not to give direct counsel or directions to their clients. Instead, they should urge the customer to solve difficulties for themself.

Rogers devised various ways for encouraging the client to voice his thoughts and feelings to encourage this type of discussion between client and therapist. Active listening is, however, one strategy. The psychotherapist avoids expressing judgmental judgments about what the client is saying, and instead tries to comprehend what they intend by describing it.

"Active listening" is a skill developed and taught in relationships. The concept is that partners can strengthen their communication by paying greater attention to each other. They will assist their partner in expressing feelings and difficulties that are bothering them, resulting in greater understanding, closeness, and, ultimately, the resolution of problems.

Active listening aims to improve communication in your relationship, but the same ideas may be used in any encounter with another person.

While you're on the phone but don't have much time to converse with somebody, active listening comes in handy. It's also an intelligent approach to convey that you're interested in what the other person is saying, rather than merely answering "yeah" or "uh-huh."

Try these methods when you're conversing with somebody and want her to feel like she's being heard:

1. Relate to the feelings expressed by the speaker. It's critical to connect with what someone else is expressing emotionally. If you're unsure about what the speaker is saying, rather than nodding or responding "uh-huh," ask questions.
2. Make the conversation about the other person. Active listening is to make everyone in the

conversation feel heard clearly. When you make it about her, she will think she has been heard, encouraging her to start listening.

Active listening is not the same as being quiet, nodding your head, and saying "uh-huh" or "mm-hmm" now and again. When you're actively listening, you're attempting to decipher what the other person is honestly saying.

The purpose of active listening is to truly hear what another person is saying and make sense of it. To do so, you must reflect what they have said to you. You can either rephrase or simply repeat what they have said to you.

However, this method can be challenging to master. If you use active listening to demonstrate that you know more about other person's sentiments and situations than they do, it's easily perceived as arrogant.

The most important thing to remember is to listen to your heart and obey your head! Your soul desires happiness while your brain sees the consequences, so pay attention to both!

Knowing what kind of individual you're looking for is a great way to guarantee you're with the right person. You can accomplish this by evaluating yourself and presenting a list of criteria for future relationships to your partner.

Rather than talking about your feelings or fighting over trivial matters, you can have discussions about what kind of person would be a good match for one another.

Listening Blocks

The philosophy and method of Blocks to Listening are designed to help you improve your listening skills. This theory's purpose is to help you acquire a set of abilities that will help you improve the quality of your relationships by allowing you to comprehend them better.

Mind Reading

Mind reading is the practice of making educated predictions about what your partner is thinking, feeling, or planning. You put way too much importance on non-verbal cues (facial expressions, tone of voice, posture) while neglecting the content of whatever they're discussing.

Mind reading can be an insidious kind of emotional neglect in a relationship. It becomes an unspoken rule that prevents couples from truly understanding one another. Mind readers focus on the imaginative rather than the obvious. They "read between the lines" and concoct explanations for their partner's actions. They imagine they know how their partner feels or thinks, allowing them to stay blissfully unaware about what's going on. It's also a symptom of low self-esteem if you can read people's minds. It occurs when you feel so unworthy of your spouse that you cannot accept their statements at face value, preferring instead to extrapolate how it makes you appear (without recognizing it). Do you downplay a compliment on your cuisine by saying, "Oh, everyone can do it"? Or do you feel compelled to say something like, "You didn't like it but you feel sorry for me since I don't know how to cook!"

Pay attention to what and how your partner says to fix this issue. Don't get mixed up between what he says and what he suggests.

Filtering

Filtering is similar to having a device that only receives specific frequencies. It's a hearing style that ignores some aspects of what the other person says. It might work OK until your partner keeps bringing up something that truly upsets you, such as alcohol abuse, your mother-in-law, or relocating out of state. Filtering isn't a conscious decision to disregard particular types of information. It merely happens to us without our knowledge. You can cease filtering by becoming more aware of what you hear in your relationship dialogues, and paying more attention to your partner.

Judging

One of the most pervasive impediments to listening is judgment. It's sneaky because it can appear that you're paying attention while you're actually labeling and judging what your partner is saying.

You don't listen to grasp what your partner says if you consider them foolish or insane. You only listen long enough to come up with new ways to back up your claims. When you characterize your partner as lazy, you only look for evidence to back up your claim.

You might think you're listening to understand your partner, but if the goal is to show how incorrect they are, you're not listening.

However, listening is one of the most challenging skills to master in a relationship. Many individuals have never learned to listen, preferring instead to criticize or judge. Patience and a willingness to understand another person's point of view are required when listening.

It takes time and it works! Start with these three principles if you're not used to listening:

1. Show your spouse that you care about what they have to say by sincerely wanting to hear what they say.
2. Be open to new facts that may persuade you to reconsider your position, even if you don't want to listen to them.
3. Don't pass judgment on your partner while speaking; instead, refrain from interrupting and going into your own story.

Daydreaming

When you're daydreaming, you're usually not thinking about your lover. Work, a hobby, or maybe another person could be on your mind. Daydreaming may appear harmless—and it feels perfect; but it can put your relationship under strain. If your thinking constantly sidetracks you, then your closest friends and family may feel insignificant and ignored.

If you spend too much time daydreaming about negative parts of your life, it might become a problem. Everyone has anxieties, but it can be tough to break free from them if you concentrate on them for an extended amount of time. When you finally snap out of it, your partner may become upset or frustrated with you because they think something is wrong. It's critical to address these concerns; if you don't, daydreaming will only become a more significant issue for both of you.

Sparring

Sparring might be beneficial in the early stages of a relationship. Sparring may bring two individuals closer together as they work out the "rules." It can also be helpful when one partner decides to take a significant step forward, but the other is hesitant or opposed. Sparring is effective for a while, but it eventually becomes problematic. Your partner does not feel heard and understood when you limit. Sparring devolves into a debate—or, worse, a war—in which everyone loses.

Sparring isn't listening; it's establishing the plan. Sparring is when you use your words to win the argument rather than convey what's actually on your mind. Since you're trying to prove something rather than getting something straight in your mind, you could become even more entrenched in your opinion. And suppose you don't receive what you want. In that case, you typically blame your partner rather than taking accountability for how difficult it is to express yourself openly about your needs and desires. Your partner might do the same thing, resulting in you blaming one another for everything (which means nothing).

Being Right

Being correct is one of the most typical roadblocks to listening. The concern that if you open yourself up to hear another person's viewpoint you may compromise your perspective, lies at the root of this barrier. To avoid this setback, you may even lie or misrepresent what you hear to support your point of view. Being correct is not an issue when it comes to stuff like asking for instructions or other practical matters. This thing becomes an issue regarding opinions and topics with solid emotional undertones. Being correct prevents communication by raising defenses against hearing anything that makes you feel exposed.

When you become protective, all you're thinking about is protecting yourself from any notion that you're not flawless. Assume your husband suggests something along these lines: "I believe we should sell our yacht. Last week, I caught two monster catfish, and we still have plenty of food in the freezer." He would not recommend getting rid of the boat if he was only concerned with facts and figures.

Listening blocks can be overcome by employing the following strategies:

Strategies for Overcoming Listening Blocks

Pay Attention To One Another

The listener must pay attention to what their partner says without interrupting them. Wait until the other individual has finished speaking before making remarks or asking questions. If you have anything to say, start writing it down and come back to it at a later date. If you don't understand something or disagree with your partner, seek clarification rather than arguing about it.

Take Some Time To Pamper Yourself

You may feel tired after hearing your partner's views, so take a while for yourself. This will help you regain strength and power for the next task of greater understanding of your partner.

Psychological Impact of Listening

Things can get complex in a relationship, and you may feel as if your partner is disregarding you. It can make you upset and irritated with your partner. If this situation arises, there are options for dealing with it.

To help you cope, keep in mind that having listened to your partner can have a significant psychological impact at times. If your partner understands how important it is for them to listen too, they are more inclined to try.

In any relationship, listening is among the most crucial communication skills. We are constantly conversing, or more accurately, exchanging data. Whether you realize it or not, your relationship is based on how well you listen to one another and act on that information.

The state of a relationship is greatly influenced by the ability to listen. It also enables us to learn a great deal more about the person with whom we are conversing. You'll be able to communicate with them more effectively and appropriately once you've learned this.

In daily life, you rely heavily on listening. It's a cornerstone of all human interactions. When you're talking to someone, you naturally listen for key phrases that will help you react accordingly to what they're saying.

Listening has tonal elements that help us decipher what has been said afterward. You observe your partner's facial expressions, body language, and other nonverbal signals for extra information when you listen.

By following their body language, you can determine whether they are frustrated, joyful, mad, or indifferent. It's like you can understand your partner's inner thoughts and feelings by noticing their body tone and language once they talk.

For instance, suppose your partner arrives back late at night again, grumbling about traffic and enraged. You've heard their voice and fully comprehend what they are saying, but instead of responding warmly, you become argumentative.

Active Listening

Active listening is a type of communication that puts the other person first. It entails paying attention to non-verbal signals and modifications in voice style, while being conscious about what the other person says and how they say it.

Effective listening strives to understand, rather than just agree with the speaker's point of view. In a relationship, listening skills are useful since they allow you to genuinely understand your spouse and create a high level of trust. Active listening in a relationship not only helps you deal with conflicts more successfully, but also ensures that you have a complete understanding of your partner's side of the argument before attempting to resolve it.

Active listening is most effective when both people speak in "I" declarations instead of "you" statements. Rather than saying, "You never pay any attention to me," try something like, "I feel unwanted when we're talking." Instead of taking offense at what they may interpret as a personal insult, this tends to encourage your partner to consider their feelings on the matter.

With practice, active listening becomes easier. Here are some suggestions:

1. Make direct eye contact with them when they speak so that you can see their nonverbal cues and hear their phrases. It exhibits that you are genuinely interested in their emotions and what they suggest.
2. Pay attention to what they are saying instead of being disturbed by what's happening around you. Whether other people start communicating or the television is on, make a concerted effort to block out the distractions and stay focused on what your partner is saying.

3. Don't pass judgment. If you have any preconceived notions after hearing your partner speak, wait until they are finished before reacting, so they don't feel attacked or misinterpreted.
4. Ask questions to clarify matters. To promote open dialogue, take the time to understand what your partner is saying and why it's essential to them. "Are these emotions regarding your connection with your dad?" or, "Are these emotions about your connection with your father?"

Reciprocal Communication

Reciprocal communication occurs when two people speak, listen, and communicate with each other in a way that they both understand. It isn't just one partner talking while the other sits back and listens. Although it may appear to be a simple task, communication is one of the most challenging aspects of any relationship.

Many factors can lead to problems with reciprocal communication, including a lack of loyalty, suspiciousness, frustration, and so on. Whatever the reason, reciprocity is an essential part of effective communication and will help your relationship succeed.

Listening and fully comprehending whatever the other person says is crucial to reciprocal communication. All of your communication efforts will be in vain if you are still unable to pay any attention. Everyday communication also necessitates clear communication so that everyone can comprehend what you're trying to say.

In a relationship, these are the main Reciprocal Communication Techniques:

1. Be genuine and open to being vulnerable. When you're honest with yourself, you're also honest with your partner.
2. When you communicate genuinely with your partner, you are honest and open with them. When you're sensitive, you say what you're thinking, irrespective of how it might impact you or your relationship.
3. First, seek to comprehend, then to be taught. This is critical in any relationship, such as intimate relationships. Unless you tell somebody else, how do you know they understand what you want? They won't be capable of giving you whatever you want if they don't know whatever you want from them – and your partner won't be able to determine what they want from you.
4. Actively listen and then reflect. Both people must be active listeners – but not too busy! – for interaction to work both ways. When someone else is speaking, active listening requires not

interrupting them with your personal view or replying until they are done speaking. Then, briefly rephrase what they've said to ensure that the other person's message came correctly. They will feel appreciated as a result of this.

Ways For Improving Communication

It's a two-way street when it comes to relationships. From a loving relationship to friendships and family relationships, any relationship requires effective communication. Both parties with a happy connection are ready to listen and share their opinions, emotions, and worries on various topics.

When this flow of communication is disrupted, trouble ensues. It prevents the parties from resolving issues and can lead to negative emotions, leading to harmful behaviors like lying or cheating.

Here are a few pointers to help you improve your communication in any relationship:

Be Forthright And Truthful

Avoid evasive responses and equivocation. If there is a problem, be honest with your partner. The sooner you bring it up, the more time you'll have to work this out together.

Things that could hurt your partner's feelings should not be hidden. If you don't feel like telling your partner straight what's going on, write it down in an email or letter instead. Then, instead of dodging the subject or trying to pretend that nothing happened, make sure your partner gets to read it and reacts.

Be Courteous And Respectful

Being cruel or insulting to your partner will only make them defensive, making them less likely to discuss their genuine emotions and thoughts with you, especially if they fear being mocked or judged for their beliefs.

Rather than copying, show your partner adoration by using words, making contact, appreciating, and using an act of service that is impactful to them. This type of positive encouragement will help you and your partner strengthen your relationship!

Communicate Your Emotions

Try to write down your emotions to convey them more noticeably. After you've had a chance to ponder what you'd like to say, this will help you communicate them more successfully in a face-to-face conversation.

If these emotions are emotionally damaging or crucial, rather than remaining vague and attempting to attack your partner, tell them why you feel the same way. If you don't like someone he's around from work, for example, clarify why rather than simply saying, "I don't like her."

CHAPTER 7: EXPRESS YOUR FEELINGS AND NEEDS

In a relationship, it's critical to convey your emotions and needs. Your relationship will struggle if you are frightened of being susceptible and have to hide behind a shell. You need to express yourself, as suppressing your feelings will stifle the relationship's development. For your connection to remain more vital than ever before, you must be susceptible. Vulnerability does not imply weakness or fragility; instead, it means that you can express your needs and feelings to each other.

Even if it's something you've never managed before, being able to express your emotional needs is not scary or difficult.

You could take a simple approach like this:

"Recently, I've been disappointed with our connection because I feel like I do not get any attention from you."

Or, "I'd like you to pay more attention to me."

Of course, the first noticeable thing while trying this method is how difficult and uncomfortable it feels! It's not easy to convey your emotions and needs in a relationship. Still, by concentrating on something specific rather than beating around the bush, you can make it much easier for yourself — and for your partner.

One of the most amazing feelings in the world is love between two people, but it can be challenging to express your feelings at times.

Here are a few pointers to help you communicate your feelings in a relationship:

1. Understand what you want and be genuine.
2. Be honest and open with your partner; show them how you feel and inquire about their feelings toward you.

3. Learn to listen without interrupting or attempting to solve their problems.
4. Don't wait for them to say anything before expressing yourself on a routine basis.
5. Don't take it all personally; they may be unable to think clearly.

Realization of Various Feelings in A Relationship

You will have many different kinds of relationships throughout your life. Relationships can either be excellent and healthy or toxic and unhealthy. To have a good relationship, you should learn to recognize the emotions affecting the relationship making you feel this way.

Toxic relationships make you feel hurt, angry, disappointed, or confused. Your behavior and feelings and the actions of others contribute to these feelings. If you're in a relationship, it can be challenging to see what is going on because you are so experienced in dealing with negative emotions that you begin to believe they are normal.

Suppose your substantial other had been distant with you recently, and you've been starting to feel heartbroken and turned down due to the shortage of interaction. In that case, you may be concentrating on your partner's behavior (i.e., they have been distant) rather than your acts (i.e., perhaps you have been pushing them away).

The key to recognizing your emotions is to remain as objective as possible. Ask yourself, do you feel secure, adored, and treated with respect in your relationship? If you answered yes, then congrats! You have a great relationship. If that's not the case, maybe it's time to move on.

Respect Yourself

If you don't appreciate yourself, others will find it difficult to respect you. When you're around somebody who doesn't respect you very much or who leaves you feeling terrible about yourself, it's time to go and find somebody who loves and cares about you and appreciates you for who you are on the inside and out.

Don't Accept Anything Below What You're Worth

Don't settle for table scraps when it comes to love and relationships. It's time to let go of someone who makes you feel terrible about yourself or your connection. No one should make you feel that they own you or run your life. No one has the authority to tell you what you should do with your life or decide things for you.

Love Is Compassionate

Because someone seems to like you, that doesn't give them the right to mistreat you. Love is a decision, but just because someone can choose to be with you does not mean they can take advantage of your generosity or harm you in any way.

Love Is Patient

Love isn't always simple, but if someone genuinely loves you, they'll seek to comprehend where you're coming from and work out a compromise. They certainly wouldn't expect you to be someone you aren't, and they'll want only the best for you.

Love is Selfless

Love can be selfless as well as kind and patient. When two people genuinely care about each other, they will put their own needs aside to ensure the happiness of the other. They may not receive what they desire or deserve.

Express Your Feelings

In a relationship, it's critical to express your feelings. This enables you to communicate your emotions to the other person. It helps to make both of you feel happy in your relationship. To develop genuine emotions, you must express your feelings to the other person through statements and behavior.

Being able to express your unconditional love for them helps them feel special and boosts their self-esteem. They'll realize how much you care about them and how much effort and time you put in to make them feel loved.

For a relationship to succeed, you must express your emotions. As a result, if you want your relationship to succeed, you must be able to communicate your feelings clearly to your partner. You can create a solid and long-lasting relationship by doing so.

Here are some pointers to consider if you want to express your feelings in a relationship:

Consider What You Truly Desire

You must know whatever you want to say in order to express yourself adequately. It will be best for the both of you if your opinions on the particular issues that disturb you are more explicit.

Do Not Become Enraged Easily

You must keep in mind that everything is not as monochrome as it appears. Things are frequently far more complex than they appear at first glance, leading to erroneous presumptions and judgments. This problem quickly makes it more difficult for both of you to recognize and express yourselves. That is why controlling your rage is crucial for saving your relationship.

Recognize The Importance Of Your Relationship To You

Understanding how much your partner means to you and how essential your connection is to your day-to-day life is one thing that could make you able to express yourself a lot more easily. This understanding will keep you going when you're feeling down and would like to give up, and it will reassure you about why you love them much in the first place.

Frequently Share Photos And Videos

We often don't realize how much we miss somebody until we see pictures of them in our inbox, Facebook, or Snapchat. You could also send short videos of yourself speaking or singing to your partner, which will be entertaining for both of you to watch when you are physically separated from each other.

Script Your Needs

If you're in a relationship, you'll want to learn how to script your requirements. The expression "ignorance is bliss" may be genuinely the case almost constantly, but not in this situation. Disregarding your partner's needs and wanting them to know what you're thinking without communication will only lead to disappointment.

The key to scripting your needs is to communicate your thoughts to your partner without trying to sound angry or accusatory. Don't chastise them about it. Keep in mind that each relationship is different, and what works for one couple might not even work for another. Try something different if what you're doing isn't continuing to work.

Scripting can express how you feel about something essential to save your relationship from anxiety. It may be easier for your partner to choose an alternative that satisfies you both or, at the very least, avoid doing anything that will put you on opposite sides if you express your desires.

It can be challenging to discern if your spouse is the one. When you're in a relationship, you might want to script your requirements to see if they're there for you. It means you'll try to set your wishes and needs behind to accomplish everything you can for your partner. Then you'll know they're the ones for you if they respond and put their desires and needs away for yours.

If someone does not respond in this way, you may be dealing with someone selfish or self-centered. You should think over your relationship with them and make sure they're the person you want to spend the rest of your life with.

If you're afraid to speak up with one another or don't know how to express yourself without actually harming the other person, seek counseling before it becomes too late.

Scrutinize Overburdening Feelings And Needs

Examine a relationship's overloading emotions and desires. If you notice that you have them, consider whether they're being satisfied correctly in your relationship. The overburdening emotions lead to anxiety in a relationship, as both partners feel tremendous pressure due to the exceeding emotional load.

Your partner's demand for constant care from you, or their desire to have complete control over every aspect of your life together, may be making you feel overburdened. You'll likely feel resentment against your partner if they don't make a conscious effort to give you the same independence they want for themselves.

If you haven't yet grown to appreciate yourself as much as they love you, you may be feeling overloaded by your desire for affection and acceptance. If this is the case, begin to practice greater self-love daily, and you'll notice that you don't require their love as much.

Since they stimulate your low self-esteem, you may feel overloaded by your partner's codependency or other feelings. If that's the case, you should work on improving your self-esteem before entering another significant relationship. It can help you feel more compassion for others and avoid taking on their issues as your own.

The key to sustaining a healthy relationship is to set reasonable expectations.

Here are some suggestions for recognizing and dealing with overburdening sentiments and needs in a relationship:

1. Make a mental note of your overburdened emotions and desires. "I need my boyfriend to hug me all night," or "My girlfriend should not be furious at me," are examples of things you demand from your spouse that they simply cannot (and should not) fulfill for you. These are unattainable targets. It will be easier to recognize and deal with them if you understand what they are.

2. Consider why your emotions are getting the best of you. What are some of the likely causes for these ideas to be running through your mind? Do you feel as if your partner is ignoring you? Do you have the impression that they no longer have time for you? Do you have a concern about something? You can take steps to remedy the problem by identifying the source of the issue.

3. Set limits with your partner, so you don't overburden them with your wants and desires. For instance, if you require more alone time than your partner does, let them know now and again and set aside some time when they're at work. If you need extra assistance around the home, ask them to help without imposing a request stating that they're not doing enough. Setting limits will allow your partner to understand what you require and when you need it without feeling pushed or demanded.

Conveying Your Feelings To Your Partner

Talk to your partner about what's happening at the time regularly. Check in with one another frequently to see how things are going when one of you is frustrated or overwhelmed. This little care will allow you to communicate when something is a significant concern and a minor detail requiring immediate attention. You will feel the elimination of anxiety due to this little gesture.

Make time in your relationship to talk. If feasible, set aside time to chat regularly or at a specific time. If you have kids, try to speak to each other when they are awake (without disrupting the kids) so that they become accustomed to watching their parents spend time with each other without them. If this isn't feasible, schedule "couple time" for evenings or weekends when nobody else is present, and you can focus solely on one another.

Make your feelings and needs known. It's critical to express how you're feeling, even if it feels insignificant or inconvenient. You don't want the person to be caught off-guard by an emotional reaction later on if things aren't going well.

You must communicate your feelings and needs to your partner while in a relationship. You must be able to express your feelings of rage, despair, and joy without criticizing or accusing others.

You can express your sentiments and wants in the following ways:

1. Use "I" statements whenever possible. "I get upset when you..." and "I need you to..." are two examples.
2. Don't make broad generalizations. "You constantly...," "You rarely...," or "Everybody can..." are some examples.
3. Use the word "because" in your sentence. "I am disappointed because you didn't remember my birthday," for example.

4. Describe your feelings. Rather than, "Stop yelling at me!" try, "Whenever you yell at me, I become terrified."
5. Use words that are caring. "I realize that...", "It makes sense that...", and "I think that..." are other examples.
6. Be explicit about what you want to achieve. Describe the problem and how the solution would be implemented. "When we go shopping together, I think it would be beneficial if we broke up so that we might move faster," for example.

Find Out Your Partner's Needs

There are several methods for determining your partner's requirements in a relationship. You can simply question them straight about it, or you can observe their conduct to see if you can deduce any clues.

Take note of their requirements and how you might assist them. It's critical to understand how to create the most delicate possible partnership.

There are various ways to make a relationship work, but you must work on it just like anything else in life. Discovering what makes your partner happy can help you become closer and see eye to eye. You wouldn't want to push anyone away or drive them out since you ignored them.

To begin, enquire about their expectations for a relationship. Pay attention as they discuss their wants and requirements. Figure out what they hope to get out of you, as well as any concerns they could have. Do not be scared to ask questions to clarify any misunderstandings with your thoughts. In a serious, romantic relationship, they should be willing to inform you precisely what they require.

Once you've figured out what they're looking for, surprise them with something unique that meets their requirements. The work begins because taking care of somebody else's needs and wishes takes time and effort. But if you truly love one other, this shouldn't be a problem and will simply strengthen your bond.

Here are some pointers to help you move your relationship forward:

- Your partner may not immediately tell you if they are dissatisfied with the relationship. They may feel self-conscious or anxious about speaking it out loud. Instead, they'll emotionally or physically withdraw from you. Ask them how they think about the relationship and where they

see it heading in the future to counterbalance this.
- If your partner is dissatisfied with the way things have been going, there may be something missing that would make them happy. Perhaps they desire greater physical closeness from you or a more emotional connection. Whatever is lacking from the relationship, attempt to fill those gaps in a way that makes them content with their choice to be there for you.

Make Your Partner Comfortable With Expressing Feelings

In a relationship, it's critical to make your spouse feel at ease when expressing sentiments. It is easier than it sounds, mainly if you've known someone for an extended period and are accustomed to their conduct.

Being patient is the best policy. When you're angry, try not to say anything that will harm or insult your partner. Instead, discuss how they feel when they are upset with you. Learning to recognize and deal with your partner's emotions constructively will help you both work toward joy in your relationship.

Both participants in a relationship must feel free to express their emotions. If one partner is hesitant to express their sentiments, the other must ensure nothing is wrong with them. This hesitation could be due to previous encounters with persons who have injured them so that a person does not feel at ease sharing their thoughts.

Expressing to your partner how you think about them and what you want out of the relationship is crucial for establishing trust and closeness, which are essential components of a good relationship. One of the critical parts of every relationship is communication.

The following are the most effective strategies to urge your partner to share their feelings:

1. When starting a discourse about feelings, be cautious. You should not begin to talk to them if you notice your partner is preoccupied or distracted by something. It's probably best to wait until they are more comfortable and have some time for you. It's the same if you notice your partner is in a terrible mood and refuses to talk about it. It is preferable to postpone such discussions to a later date.
2. If you believe your partner is irritated, don't say anything that will aggravate them further. This

rule should apply to both men and women, but women should exercise more caution in this situation because they can easily harm their partner's sentiments without realizing it.

CHAPTER 8: CHANGING YOUR AVERSIVE STRATEGIES

In a relationship, the honeymoon phase is full of illusions. It is a hologram of two individuals becoming one by merging their love. Their love is a satisfaction to each other and is an important need for humans.

But, as time passes, that illusion starts to fade. The image of an all-encompassing unity free from pain and sorrow is now replaced with the knowledge that both have very different needs. And sometimes the needs are not just different; they are opposite to each other. This kind of disillusionment that follows the shattered fantasy of the perfect couple is an unavoidable phase.

Everyone wants different things, and there are only a few people whose likes and dislikes are the same. Sometimes, people very close to each other pull in different directions just because of their different needs, and perfectly matched couples have conflicts in their needs. Dealing with problems that arise because of a conflict in needs is best done by using constructive methods.

Against the conflicts, the strategies that you will use will help you determine the satisfaction level of your relationship. There are two different types of strategies: healthy strategies and aversive strategies. Both of these strategies are opposite to each other.

In healthy strategies, partners compromise with each other's needs and acknowledge the importance of each other's needs. And in aversive strategies, one partner forces the other partner to give up or give in on what they want by using fear and shame.

The results of aversive strategies are awful and become the reason for anxiety in the relationship. And your partner will be intimidated or hurt after giving you what you want from him. Soon your partner becomes inured, numb, deeply alienated, or rebellious. Trust and intimacy are the base of a perfect relationship, but these are replaced with resistance, detachment, and anger. So, to get what you want from your partner, you have to pay a high price. Like, the frustration and anxiety of your partner will increase and become the reason for ending your relationship.

Eight Aversive Strategies

This chapter will identify eight different aversive strategies. Once you identify them, you will eradicate any of these strategies from your behavior if you are using any. Below are eight aversive strategy methods that you should avoid:

Discounting

Your partner will get the idea that their needs are not critical. You lack the legitimacy, importance, and magnitude of their needs. The main goal of this strategy in agreeing is to embarrass them.

"For God's sake, Honey, you have spent the entire day at home watching Oprah. Can you tell me why you want me to pay the bills?" (Overall message: My desire to rest overcomes your desire to avoid doing this work.)

"Every time we go to meet your brother, all you two do is sit around and play backgammon. You do not even go out of the house for a breath of fresh air. When we go to my mother's house, at least people talk to one other. It is more than simply games; it is a true family atmosphere." (Basic message: seeing my mother is more important because we do something meaningful and genuine.)

Withdrawal

In this strategy, you are messaging your partner to do what you want threatening that or else you will leave. Withdrawal and abandonment threats are very frightening to every partner. Sometimes, your partner will give up and do what you want him to do.

"If you cannot pick me up, I think this relationship should be over." (The basic message here is that you will be alone if you will not pick me up).

So here is another reaction that a husband had when he came to know that his partner had a college reunion for which she had to go to Boston for three days. Husband to his wife, "Go and do whatever you want to do; I will stay here and will watch TV tonight, will see you later. Do not hang around." (Basic message here is that if you go, I will check out emotionally for a bit. I am not going to be intimate.)

Sometimes a deep freeze in emotions take place because of this withdrawal. It is sometimes a cold gap. However, it can take away precious things: the feeling of being connected with your partner, the essence of a relationship.

Threats

The primary strategy here is to make sure that you harm your partner.

"I am done with you being all high and mighty and shit. There is no job that you think is good for you. You can take this job because I am done with covering for your pathetic career." (Basic message: You will do what I say, or I'll bad-mouth you.)

"Ok fine, I will not demand this from you again (a specific sexual act). I might ask someone else." (Basic message: You should satisfy my sexual urges, or I'll have a sexual relationship with someone else.)

According to this, one partner tries to control the other person by hurting them. It is a do-or-die strategy that partners will either get what they want or lose all they have.

Blaming

The main objective of this strategy is to make your partner believe that your needs are your partner's fault.

"If you had shown your genuine self, I would not have been in an emotional void like this. I am simply asking, what is going in your head?" (Basic message: It's your fault I feel like this.)

Or, another objective is to make your partner think their needs are their fault. "You would not have to face such a situation if you had listened to me and taken the kids on a streetcar while going to the zoo. There would not have been any breakdown in the car, and you wouldn't have to struggle to get it fixed." (Basic message: You should fix the problem as you were the one who created it.)

It shows that you expect your partner to solve a problem if you blame them.

Belittling/Denigrating

This strategy works by making your partner feel stupid if they have any need you do not have.

"Why are you always asking to visit the lake?" (Basic message: Your desire is foolish.)

"Do your friends have anything sensible to talk about? Can we be friends with someone who is not always talking about who is having fun at the club or which are the newest designer sunglasses?" (Basic message: You should leave your friends as they do not have any value.)

In this strategy, shame and fear make other partner feel stupid and devalued.

Guilt-Tripping

This strategy conveys that if your partner has a desire that does not align with your wishes, they are a moral failure as they do not support your desires and wants.

"I am the one who keeps this house running 24/7, and you are not willing to spend just twenty minutes to fix the oven door. I think the only thing you want to do is lie on that couch."(Basic message: It is unfair if you want to rest.)

"I am always willing to do whatever you ask sexually, but if I ask you to dress in a certain way to make me feel good, you say it's weird or embarrassing." (Basic message: It is unfair if you say no to me.)

Derailing

When your partner starts talking about their needs, you change the conversation, showing that they are not worthy of being discussed.

"I know that you need more time for yourself, off from the kids. Both of us are busy. Ok, listen, there are only two days left in Hornblower Society's lecture for which I still have to prepare. By the way, is my suit back from the laundry? And yes, let Susie know I want to see a perfect score in her spelling test."(Basic Message: My problems are way more important than anyone else's.)

"You are not able to give time to your music? Consider joining a club. There is chaos going on in Salvadore's school. The teacher who was teaching language has left, while the algebra teacher suffers from Lyme's Disease. And one of the students and his parents were hit by one of the aides..."(Basic Message: Your music is not a big deal.)

Taking Away

In this strategy, the partner takes away some pleasure or support. In short, you take away something your partner enjoys.

"Hiking does not feel interesting anymore, and I am not in the mood for that either," the partner said in a cruel way when the other partner was reluctant to buy a new computer. (Basic message: You will not have any fun with me if you do not get a PC.)

"I think everyone should do their own laundry from now on in this house. It would be best if you were taking care of yourself, Peter." This happened after Peter refused to check his wife's car for making weird noises. (Basic message: If you refuse me, I will punish you.)

The Harms Of Aversive Strategies

Aversive strategies harm the relationship by making both people become frustrated and enraged, which leads to anxiety. Even your partner will feel worthless because of the frustration and rage because of your behavior. It then becomes the reason to end your relationship, even in minor conflicts.

The Cold Effect Of Humiliation

Belittling is all about making your partner feel silly and weird with your behavior and words. You think it is inappropriate that your partner has different requirements and necessities.

For example, there is a PTA meeting, and you do not want to go there. Instead of just denying it, you told your partner that it is just a waste of time. It will make them just hurt, and things will become odder between you. Or maybe you did not say anything about the meeting but just went to your work. This will also make the situation worse.

Loss of Connection

The other strategy is to make the partner do what others want them to do. The consequence is that this destroys something valuable, which is the backbone of any relationship or connection between partners.

For example, your partner wants to place a desk under the tree. You made a statement that it is ridiculous to put the desk there, instead of telling them to change where it is. This will make the situation worse and cold. Or maybe you make your partner follow your instructions even about these little things, or say they can leave the house if they don't agree. This will not make the relationship work, but it may make your partner want to move to another place if it is happening continuously.

Loss of Trust

Suppose you are accusing your partner of belittling your necessities and their desires. It will make the relationship weak and cold if you blame only one person for everything. If your partner gets the blame for a priority, necessity, or desire, they will get offended. It will result in a situation where your partner will stop putting them in front of you. They will stop telling you about every small decision and detail about their life. It will lead to a loss of trust in a relationship.

Long-Lasting Scars

There can be long-lasting scars in the people you care about from aversive behavior and in the relationship you want to keep the most. Aversive strategies can potentially ruin relationships. Your partner will find it hard to trust you and will feel insecure. It will be difficult for your partner to speak honestly and comfortably with you when offended or enraged.

Aversive strategies result in physical, mental, or verbal abuse. No one accepts any form of bullying or harassment in a relationship. Abuse can be inappropriate; speaking badly to the other person, physically hurting and harming them, or humiliating them.

End of A Relationship

Aversive strategies are deadly harmful to relationships. If you are responding in rage and anger, even in a situation where you can end the discussion very calmly, it will destroy the relationship. Your partner may leave you because of the melodrama happening daily.

If your partner is angry, you will be too if it frequently happens. There could be two options - either both will shout at each other, or will ignore each other. When neither partner can control their temper, a minor conflict could quickly become a major one. It also extends the range of the dispute further. It leads to anxiety for both of you and then ends the relationship destructively.

Identification Of Aversive Behavior

Regardless of the perfection of the relationship, there can be chances for the couples to have different interests and conflicting demands. However, the most challenging task for couples is to handle and solve conflict constructively. But aversive behavior only ruins the relationship, just as rage and anger ruin the moment of discussion and have long-lasting, deadly effects.

In productive strategies, compromises are emphasized, and every interest and requirement of each partner is considered and respected. In an aversive approach, anger, fear, humiliation, and shame urge your partner to make them give in or surrender according to your order.

The outcomes of aversive strategies are destructively cold. Even the worth and effectiveness of the relationship lose their value and power over time. As a result of their intervention, people become insensitive, aggressive, and emotionally unstable. Anger, coldness, or opposition end up replacing closeness and trust. They ruin the relationship and, at last, destroy the relationship badly.

The following are the signs of aversive behavior and their deadly effects on relationships.

Disregarding

Suppose you disregard your partner's desires by thinking that their requirements, needs, or demands are not worthy. If you remember that your needs are essential and humiliate other people for agreeing with a statement, it will not make the relationship worthy, but cold.

Threatening

This is giving threats to them or doing them harm if they will not do whatever you want. As a means of force, one partner intends to harm the other physically.

Criticizing

Only one person is criticized in a relationship. One partner will always blame the other partner, whatever one does. It leads to even blaming the other partner for their own needs or desires. If you did something wrong, then your partner will fix it, and if they did something wrong, it is still their fault and they have to fix it.

Controlling By Fear And Shame

This happens when you make your partner feel guilty by having different desires than you. Your partner wants to do something, but you do not, and you start insulting him for having such a stupid desire - this is inappropriate in a relationship. Your partner's desire controls you using fear and insults, so that they give up their needs and demands because of the fear of you devaluing them.

Ignorance

It would be best not to believe that only your needs, desires, and issues are worth discussing. The needs and issues of your partner are important and fun to discuss too. Not talking about your partner's needs may jeopardize your relationship. Even in extreme circumstances, your partner will not listen to your concern if it occurs repeatedly.

Changing Aversive Behavior

Aversive strategies are deadly for relationships and invariably destroy relationships. One can always get what one wants forcefully, but the consequences are always bitter and cold. It is necessary to consider what behavior you need to show according to the situation for saving relationships.

By focusing on changing the following aversive behavior, you may effectively prevent damage to your relationship. Aversive behaviors you need to change are: threats, judgments, disrespect, and ignorance.

Don't pressure your partner by threatening to harm yourself if they don't do whatever you want. When you threaten to hurt yourself, your partner will manipulate you at that time and agree on whatever you want, but this will end up backfiring in the future.

Don't say: "If you loved me, you would do this for me." Instead say: "If you want to do it, then you can. I'm not going to make you do it."

Try to accept a "no" in answer by your partner even if you don't like to accept it, or it's difficult for you. Upholding the answer "no" will show your partner that they have a right to speak their thoughts in the relationship. Later, your partner will respond to your decision with all their heart.

Avoid making fun of your partner's decisions, and don't put them down. Don't portray your partner as self-centered, immature, or unpredictable. Avoid criticizing your partner. The demands and decisions of your partner are equally as significant as yours.

Avoid saying, "It's your fault that we got in that fight." But instead, say: "We are in this together. I'm here for you. We'll sort out this together."

Your relationship will convert to a game if it's full of aversive behavior. You feel like winning or losing the argument. You need to understand others' needs and desires too. A relationship can be destroyed by constantly forcing your partner to agree to your orders or needs. In a relationship, you also have to sacrifice your desires, needs, and requirements for the comfort of others. It would help if you kept in mind that your comfort, needs, and desires have the same importance. Compromise is necessary for the working of every relationship. Otherwise, your relationship can end badly.

Don't disrespect your partner verbally, emotionally, or physically. Your partner will get frustrated by this, leading to anxiety and then destroying the relationship. Physical abuse includes making funny expressions, rolling your eyes, mocking, or chuckling. Avoid doing this.

Don't move away or end discussions immediately. Do not tell your partner whatever they're saying is worthless, or that you don't bother with their feelings and emotions.

When you and your partner find a decision point, it's necessary to listen and understand what they're saying, not what you want to hear. Try to understand your partner's point of view too when making decisions. Establishing strings of connection with your partner is essential to overcome your anxious thoughts. That requires paying close attention with an open mind and heart to what your partner says.

CHAPTER 9: ANGER MANAGEMENT

Whenever a relationship breaks up or starts to worsen, the first thing that goes at the top of the reasons list is anger. Anger ruins most relationships and bonds, but a romantic relationship is shattered in an instant if you cannot keep your anger in check. That is why anger management is vital for saving your relationship and peace as a couple.

Uncontrolled and unmanaged anger changes the dynamics of any situation you face in a relationship, harming your understanding and bond. That is why learning to deal with your rage while being in a relationship is essential. Even if one partner has anger issues, one should realize that the anger, when not reined in, makes it hard to keep the relationship together.

How Anger Affects A Relationship

It is normal to have problems in a relationship or marriage, as winning a relationship has almost the same odds as a coin flip. That is why a little bit of anger or conflict is okay if you keep it checked or under control. But troubles start when any partner keeps letting out anger and expressing it intensely every time.

Anger is all about control and keeping the signs of irritation at a minimum. When you get angry at your partner, it feels like you are trying to solve the anxiety in your relationship by gaining control over your partner. The signs of such behavior can be angry facial expressions or angry speech. Both men and women use anger to control each other to maintain their superiority. And this kind of anger is the main trigger for fights and anxiety which ultimately sabotages your bond.

Keeping the anger inside causes smothering and makes you submissive and compromising. This approach is also unhealthy, because it makes you tired of your relationship. It is okay to express your anger and emotions once in a while, but ensure they stay within limits. The problem arises when you are getting angry with your partner often. Habitual anger shows that you have become controlling in your relationship.

Sometimes, you use your anger as a tool to solve other problems in the relationship. When you already have anxiety as a couple, there will be so much frustration that you may channel into anger. But a repeated show of anger signifies how controlling and manipulative you are. This habitual anger weakens the equality and sense of freedom in a relationship. Your partner gets the idea that you no longer care for them or your relationship. It leads to so many misunderstandings and conflicts that keep piling up, worsening the anxiety.

You need to control your anger before enjoying the freedom and understanding in the relationship. It widens the gap between you and your partner, as your communication becomes weak after repetitive conflicts and issues. This rage causes the connection to wither in the vine, and eventually, it dies, which is a traumatic outcome.

History

Anger management is a term used by therapists, psychotherapists, and counselors to assist people in better regulating their rage and channeling this in a way that does not damage them or others.

Anger management is a program that teaches people how to regulate their anger and manage it in healthy and constructive ways.

On the other hand, the hydraulic model has shown to be unnecessarily basic. Anger does not just accumulate, and releasing does not always bring significant effects.

There are better methods to deal with rage, which we'll discuss in a moment. But first, consider why always expressing anger might be detrimental.

Burgoon and Hale (1980) discovered that people who want to express their anger do not have a lower cardiovascular risk than those who show their wrath.

The group that expressed their rage, on the other hand, had a faster heart rate. This shows, among many other things, that there is tension connected with keeping in one's sentiments instead of letting them out.

Sorkin et al. also showed the physiological implications of repressing rage (1982). Another research compared persons who yelled to those who did not, and they found that those who shouted had more significant blood pressure than those who did not cry while burning off their anger. Furthermore, after venting, individuals were less able to manage their blood pressure in the face of various types of stress. According to research, releasing anger does not always result in catharsis or diminish its intensity.

There are also some case studies of cognitive-behavioral therapy for anger management. One is a product of a successful treatment program in Hawaii (1977). The researchers discovered that their customers were frequently furious with themselves. They were angry with themselves when they failed to reach high standards and were mad when they felt wrong about not meeting the expectations of others, such as parents or spouses. They were angry with themselves for being unable to regulate their aggressive tendencies. Sometimes people direct their rage at specific persons, such as parents, but they might also direct it towards themselves. This is an example of self-directed anger, a cognitive distortion.

Keep Track Of Your Anger

Before you start changing your furious behavior, you must first understand what is causing it. To do so, you must first know how your anger manifests itself. You will learn more about what causes your angry feelings and behaviors if you keep an Anger Assessment Record.

You may begin to work on your anger once you've recognized your triggers. The first step is to distinguish between the emotion of anger and the conduct you engage in when you're furious. For example, if you react angrily to a situation and feel guilty about it, your anger has most likely transformed into aggressiveness. Anger is not inherently harmful; it is violent action that ensues which causes issues.

To make any changes in your feelings or behavior, you must first comprehend the source of your rage. For the next seven to fourteen days, keep an Anger Assessment Record. Write down what happened objectively and behaviorally when annoyed with your partner in the Event column. Make a list of the things that enraged you and what they said or did.

Next to this, write how your anger makes you feel. What were your emotions like? What emotions were you having at the time? What were you telling yourself and others about yourself? Fill in the blanks beneath this column with your thoughts about these feelings.

You'll see a pattern in your rage as you keep track of it. In other circumstances, you may just have enough time to finish the first column before realizing you are upset. In other cases, you may realize that the previous incident was very neutral, but something irritated you about how your spouse stated or did it.

What would your partner say about what happened? If they say, "You were so upset when I told you I'd be working late again today and wouldn't be able to take out the garbage or clean up the kitchen that I feared we'd fight. But when I apologized for not having enough time to accomplish everything, you accepted it and said alright. But then, as I went to work, you slammed the door in my face without even saying goodbye." What impression do you get from this description? Your spouse claims to be astonished by your rage since they felt horrible about not accomplishing it and thought they had appropriately apologized. They anticipated you to reciprocate with goodwill—that you would accept their apology without more questions or demands, and simply say goodbye.

Note The Triggers

A mixture of factors can trigger anger. Some people have a short fuse, while others have a long fuse. In any event, anger is an issue in a relationship.

The first step in regulating your anger is understanding why you feel upset. Are you quickly enraged when anything goes wrong in your relationship? When do you get enraged? What irritates you? Make a list of the relationship's triggers so you can avoid or deal with them when they arise.

When attempting to manage your anger, be truthful about what causes it so that you can focus on coping with it. For example, if an argument constantly ends with one person claiming, "You rarely listen," this could be resolved by hearing more and not taking everything so personally.

Be honest with yourself about what will help you control your anger. Sometimes it's hard to change a situation, but that doesn't imply there's nothing you can do. If debating just makes matters worse, don't argue. If pounding walls is your thing, go ahead and knock yourself out.

You don't have to get rid of your trigger thoughts; instead, you can manage them.

Here are a few ways for dealing with the two primary types of trigger thoughts:

Thoughts for the Day

Urgent thoughts, such as, "What if I can't pay my expenses this month?" cause anxiety about the future. Alternatively, "What if I get a panic attack at work?" You may handle these ideas by staying in the current moment and concentrating on practical solutions. Remind yourself that you have an illness that is unexpected but treatable. Then consider how you'd manage a worst-case scenario, like falling behind on your payments, if this arose. Would you go to any lengths to pay them? If not, take steps now to avoid being caught off-guard later.

Distorted Thoughts

When you have distorted ideas, you are more likely to become angry because you blame others and make expectations out of proportion to the circumstance, such as, "My partner should never leave dirty dishes in the kitchen!" You may regulate these ideas by analyzing the evidence for and against these ideas and then using critical thinking abilities such as posing questions, keeping records, and seeking alternate opinions.

Combat The Blamers

Blaming is a form of expressing one's rage and dissatisfaction. If you blame people for making you furious instead of understanding that your responses are the issue, you're probably in a loveless marriage. Blaming the blamer allows you to avoid dealing with your anger. It is helpful to remember that two persons are participating in a conversation, and both of them may be held accountable for the rage.

Blame is frequently associated with some type of mind reading. You perceive another person's actions as having a hidden intention or significance. The most prevalent kind of mind-reading is assuming that someone did something to harm you purposely. People call others terrible, foolish, incompetent, uninformed, etc., when they think someone intentionally hurt them.

Struggling to figure out why someone did something might blind you to what they did. A spouse may spend hours figuring out why his wife looked through his wallet and discovered an unusual credit card statement. She couldn't understand why he was so upset about her innocent and naive action, which was a case of a misunderstanding about how credit card bills were going up.

One approach to dealing with this recognizes that others act for their motives, not yours.

Blamers jeopardize relationships. They create a situation where a partner is always wrong and can never win, even if their intentions are genuine. If you have a blamer in your life, you must stop the behavior before it becomes too difficult to quit.

Here are a few suggestions for dealing with and combating blame:

Don't Take A Defensive Stance

Blamers require someone to blame for everything, yet they will find something to be upset over if you debate or explain yourself. When they've finished venting, learn to acknowledge their anger without getting into a dispute and reassure them rather than reasoning with them. Let them know you're paying attention and that you're available to them.

Attempt To Comprehend The Blamer's Underlying Issues

If you believe your partner is unfairly criticizing you, take a minute to assess whether their claims are accurate.

Stress Inoculation

Relationship stress is a typical situation that may put the relationship under strain. When a problematic scenario arises, it catches you off-guard. It evokes emotions you may have never experienced before, and you aren't always sure how to respond to them. That is why stress inoculation training is required. What does stress inoculation training entail? It is a type of treatment that teaches you to do a few things to calm yourself down when you are tense or anxious, preventing those feelings from escalating into anger. When there is an issue with rage in your relationship, it is necessary to undertake stress inoculation education on yourself and your spouse.

By learning more about stress, you will better manage it. Stress manifests itself in several ways and may produce a wide range of reactions in the human body, so it's critical to understand where it originates and how it manifests itself.

You and your partner can benefit from specific cognitive-behavioral strategies. You may choose to take one of many actions. The first step is for both of you to educate yourself about stress inoculation and what it involves. This is an educational approach that will help you understand why you have rage problems in the first place. The next stage is learning how stress affects the body, mind, and behavior.

Medicine for the victim and treatment for the batterer are two parts of domestic violence therapy. The distinction between the two is that victim therapy concentrates on assisting the victim in coping with their previous abuse, and educating them on how to defend themselves in the future. The batterer's treatment focuses on modifying their abusive behavior, such as assisting them in identifying what triggers their violent episodes and then educating them on how to prevent those triggers.

Stress inoculation treatment assigns you chores, such as keeping a diary or notebook, to help you discover your emotional responses to various stimuli. This can be done to understand your triggers and create techniques for avoiding or controlling them more effectively.

As a tip, you can use these stress inoculation techniques with your spouse:

Self-Instruction

Instructing yourself to calm down is one of the most efficient strategies to bring yourself down from a high level of arousal. That's correct! You must tell yourself – aloud — that you will do it. The more forcefully you persuade yourself out of it, the more probable it is that you will relax.

Relaxing your body is a taught skill, so I'll start there. First, you must understand how to relax your muscles through diaphragmatic breathing. Diaphragmatic breathing takes slow, deep breaths from the abdomen rather than the chest. Shallow and ineffective chest breathing causes the pulse rate to increase and makes you feel vulnerable.

Even if you're enraged, it's critical not to do something that might jeopardize your relationship. People in positions of authority are more vulnerable to being dismissed for an angry outburst. Remember that rage is a secondary emotion with a hidden meaning. It's a natural method to take command of a situation. So, even if you believe you were the victim of crime or unfairness, it is sensible to find productive strategies to deal with your anger.

If you don't have a stash of tranquilizers on hand, consider any of these alternatives.

Instruct Yourself To Unwind

Take some deep breaths and convince yourself that you are going to relax. Repeat as needed. When they require aid with control, some people have positive self-talk mantras that they repeatedly repeat: "Remain calm; remain calm; remain calm," or some variant on that subject.

Assure Yourself That You Can Handle The Situation

Anger is an emotional reaction to a perceived danger or insult. When you find yourself saying, "I can't bear this!" remind yourself that you can. You can handle anything if you give yourself enough time.

Listen To Music

Researchers have shown that music's rhythm can help people calm down.

Wear Relaxing Clothing

This is an often-overlooked method of creating calm. There's a reason we sleep in our jammies. Try yoga pants or loose sweatpants if you want something a bit trendier. They allow you to breathe more easily and relax into your outfit.

Take A Hot Shower

Because the water helps release stiff muscles, a warm shower can help reduce anxiety.

Work Out

Exercise releases endorphins, which ease pain, and it also helps relieve nervousness by clearing your mind.

Cope With The Anger Of Your Partner

Anger is an emotion caused by hurt, anguish, and stress. It's not a terrible thing; it's an entirely natural human feeling that we all experience from time to time.

It is tough to deal with your partner's rage. It will undoubtedly help if you are more careful and aware of yourself in your daily life.

Trying to figure out what might irritate the person you adore isn't always straightforward, especially if you've never been in a relationship before. You might try asking those around you what they believe might irritate your partner.

Attempting to remove someone's anger is akin to trying to clear their happiness. It doesn't work, you can't do it, and it only irritates people.

So, what is the best option? How will you deal with your partner's rage?

Recognize It

The first step is to recognize that everyone gets angry and has an angry spouse at some point in their lives. So that's not unusual, and there are several ways to deal with it.

Accept That Rage Is A Natural Emotion

Don't ask yourself, "Why is he so angry?" or say, "I've never seen her like this before!" Acknowledge that they are upset and move on. You are not required to agree with all they say - acceptance is not the same as agreement.

Keep Your Cool

People feed off each other's feelings, so if they are furious, you will be upset as well if you allow yourself to become caught up in their emotions and lose your sense of serenity.

Listen

Don't disturb your partner when they are speaking. Pay close attention and attempt to grasp what they are saying. When you've finished listening to what they have to say, tell them you understand and interpret why they react the way they do.

Recognize Your Emotions

If your partner is upset, it is critical that you accept their sentiments rather than rejecting or dismissing them as foolish or stupid. You could say something like, "It sounds like you're upset about this." When discussing a topic that directly affects your partner, you may say, "I can tell that this genuinely concerns you."

Identify The Triggers Of Your Partner

It is critical to understand your partner's triggers. We all have good and negative stimuli. The negative motivation can be how you speak with your spouse. If you talk sarcastically, your spouse may be triggered and feel assaulted. This may spark an argument, potentially worsening the situation for both of you.

One of the most frequent inquiries I get from partners is, "How can I detect my partner's triggers?"

Here are some pointers to enable you to recognize and comprehend your partner's triggers.

1. Pay attention to their emotions. You may not comprehend why your spouse behaves because you are unaware of a trigger. As a result, instead of becoming sidetracked by the issue at hand, concentrate on understanding what sparked your partner's reaction and attempting to deal with it afterward.
2. For example, if you are busy with work and your partner asks you for assistance with something and you bounce right back at them without even understanding that stress from work is visible in your body language and facial expressions, your partner may feel assaulted.

3. It is critical to comprehend them. We frequently think that our partners understand what we want or feel, while we are failing to communicate appropriately. If your spouse feels ignored and unloved, you must tell them how much you love and adore them. Send a beautiful email, a love note, or a bouquet, for example, to express your feelings.
4. Some partners complain that they never get enough attention from their spouses, while others complain that they get too much all of the time. If you find yourself in either of these situations, you should talk to your spouse about it and try to understand their point of view.
5. If there are some communication issues in your relationship, don't take it so personally and instead find a way to work on it as quickly as possible; otherwise, it might lead to significant problems later. Communication is one of the most important aspects of a happy relationship.

Your Attitudes Towards The Anger Of Your Partner

Partnerships may be a source of contention. It's normal to react differently to your partner's rage than to the fury of others. Knowing these emotions and how they influence your relationship can allow you to cope with them more effectively.

Treat your relationship the same way you would a friend. Your partner is entitled to the same level of respect as everyone else in your life. If you wouldn't respond to a friend the way you do to your spouse, it's time to rethink your situation. Rather than recriminations and blaming, look for positive strategies to deal with anger.

You should not take things personally. When someone is upset with you, it does not imply that they no longer love you or are concerned about you. This suggests that the angry person's emotional outburst results from circumstances that might be modified if the angry person was aware of them. While experiencing such intense emotions, they are unable to see correctly.

When coping with your partner's rage, don't let your feelings get in the way of logic. Even if their remarks appear to be an assault, try not to respond defensively or angrily when they blow up at you. Understand that this is simply one method for some people to express themselves.

Hint: Anger isn't necessarily a bad thing, it may push you to make critical life choices. However, if you're feeling very overwhelmed by this emotion, consider obtaining help from a therapist or counselor who can teach you how to regain control of your anger and utilize it appropriately.

Practice Assertive Responses

Assertiveness is a valuable trait to develop in every relationship, not just romantic ones. It is the capacity to express your thoughts and feelings in a straightforward, direct, and honest manner.

Trying to argue with someone who should be assertive but doesn't know how will always result in complications and broken feelings.

Being assertive does not imply being confrontational or impolite; instead, it means articulating your views, needs, goals, and aspirations in such a manner that the other person understands them without feeling personally attacked.

You don't have to walk into every scenario with your guns blazing, but you may minimize confrontation by responding assertively rather than passively or aggressively.

Assertive communication consists of two steps. The first step is to explain oneself openly and honestly. This is taking in all of the facts around you attentively, and responding while respecting yourself and others. The second step is to communicate your demands without making others feel horrible about themselves or their decisions.

The Right Approach to Communicate Is to Be Assertive

Being assertive does not require being unpleasant or insulting the other person; it simply means efficiently expressing yourself. On the other hand, being aggressive suggests that you are going too far or breaching the rights of another individual. When someone acts aggressively toward you, they are also breaking your limits and seeking to exert some form of control over you. It is critical to understand how to be an aggressive communicator to avoid being controlled by others.

Probe The Criticism

You must investigate a critique of your relationship if you are in one and being criticized. If your partner is sincerely interested in you, they will be able to tell you about their concerns. "I feel like you do not believe me," they could remark, or, "You're not eager to try new things." These claims are valid, and they provide weight to the critique.

For example, when the wife says, "You don't listen when I talk," he understands she means it since she says it all the time. This does not imply that she attempts to dispute or provoke a conflict with him. The purpose of speaking these things out is to grab your attention to remedy the situation.

If your partner criticizes you for things that never happened, it's more probable that they're attempting to provoke you. "You don't do anything around the home," someone could complain, or, "I'm sick of you constantly doing that." These assertions are just false. If someone says these things over and over, it's possible they're not the ideal person for you.

TIP: Be truthful to yourself.

If you and your partner have problems, there is a problem to be fixed. First, you must determine the nature of the problem. This will aid you in locating the answer later on. To tackle the problem, you must first identify what the issue is in your relationship.

Acknowledge The Mistakes

Recognize faults in a relationship, but never bring up previous poor conduct in an argument. When you argue, you're not attempting to solve problems; you're looking to win. Bringing up prior mistakes will make your spouse defensive and unwilling to see anything other than his perspective of the story.

Coming to grips with a relationship's errors may be difficult. It's far simpler to point the finger at your partner and pledge never to make the same errors again, but this is rarely productive.

To begin forgiving someone, you must first admit their flaws as well as your own. This complex process requires reflection, but it is necessary to progress in any relationship.

Telling yourself that you will never repeat the same mistakes in future relationships is meaningless because you don't know what mistakes you'll make — or how deeply they'll influence your relationships — until they happen. If you're continuously in denial about your blunders, you'll forget the lessons you've learned from them.

Forgetting errors in relationships not only holds you back individually, but it may also harm the well-being and joy of others. You create a safe space for others to do the same by admitting your flaws.

Deflect

"Deflect" is an often-used term since it is one of the most efficient responses to disagreement or criticism. Instead of becoming defensive when confronted with a problem or complaint, you should try to solve the problem. You accept criticism and then "deflect" it by shifting the attention back.

You can also use this strategy to "agree" with criticism in a way that doesn't make you feel like you're losing an argument.

When someone brings up a concern with you, simply respond with, "You're correct." This appears to be too simple to be accurate, but it works like a charm. Accept what they have to say and move on. You've handled their complaint and demonstrated that you hear them just by expressing those words. That alone will put an end to most arguments!

By agreeing with whatever the other person says, you can deflect their anger and criticism.

There might be a valid reason why you find yourself deflecting or dodging disagreement in a love relationship. You may be unconsciously aware that you are not prepared to cope with your partner's emotional baggage from the past. It is easy to become aggressive, defensive, and nasty when emotionally heated. This might lead to you not speaking what you truly want to say, leading to unwarranted bitterness. Before you realize it, your relationship has changed direction and may be over.

Deflecting examples:

1. You've had a difficult day at work, and your partner expresses concern about something. You respond by saying, "Oh well, don't let it get to you," since it's simpler than addressing the matter and reaching a settlement.
2. You've been seeing someone for a few months when they tell you about a previous relationship that ended in disaster owing to their infidelity. You respond, "That was a long time ago," instead of attempting to understand how they feel about it now.
3. You are married for a while, and your spouse mentions how they feel a lack of closeness with you. You attempt to change the subject since you don't know how to address this issue.

Limit The Damage

If your partner is controlling, deceptive, volatile, or violent, you may limit the damage in your relationship by declining to stay in situations. You may also limit the damage in your relationship by refusing to remain in cases. Sometimes individuals are intentionally abusive, but most of the time, it is just how someone reacts when they are worried or intimidated.

When you confront the individual and try to persuade them to stop, they may accuse you of assaulting or even beating them, claiming that it was not their fault.

Trying to cope with an angry individual who blames you for everything may be incredibly confusing and hurtful. Setting limits and boundaries to avoid getting sucked into the dispute is the most excellent method to defend oneself. After all, you can't alter anybody else; the only thing you can do is look after yourself. If your partner becomes furious at you for establishing limitations, this might indicate that he attempts to control you.

If the verbal abuse persists after you have asked him to stop, it may be time to divorce or split up. Discussing your worries with a counselor or clergyperson might assist you in making this decision.

Limiting the damage in a relationship may be accomplished by assuring yourself that your partner is merely sharing their viewpoint, and it is only one. Even though you love your partner and want to satisfy them, it is still only one person's perspective. You can just express your dissatisfaction by stating something like, "What do you think? That is not something I intended to accomplish." If your partner doesn't stop nagging you about anything, say something like, "I understand what you're saying, but I believe I'll stick to my plan." Remember that no one is flawless.

Many of us want our marriages to be flawless in everything we do, and when we fall short of our own or our partner's standards, we might feel awful about ourselves. This, however, does not make you a nasty (or inept, selfish, or foolish) person. It simply implies you're human and doing your best. Everybody makes errors and has weaknesses.

This is similar to when someone says something harmful to you, such as, "You're selfish," or, "You rarely think about anybody but yourself." The truth is that none of us are flawless, and we do not always put others first.

CHAPTER 10: THE HARM OF "SHOULDS"

When one person attempts to impose their ideas, expectations, and aspirations on the other, "shoulds" can cause harm in a relationship. The notion that you should be allowed to do anything you would like in your relationship is the most typical example. You should never be forced to make a compromise.

Your lover is either terrible or incorrect if you are forced to do things, and they do not truly love you. This attitude is entirely wrong! It's not only unjust, but it also causes pain for both partners in the relationship.

When one person's wants are consistently satisfied while the other's are continually neglected or rejected, anger quickly arises. It may begin as a minor inconvenience, but the pressure may gradually build to the point where you want out of the relationship.

The term "should" has no inherent meaning in a relationship. "You should do more around here," one partner would say to the other. "YOU'RE THE ONE WHO SHOULD BE DOING MORE AROUND HERE," is a frequent response.

The suggestion is that one or both spouses may be doing something incorrectly or insufficiently. Each partner feels accused and defensive, which leads to a power conflict rather than a helpful solution.

It will have a negative impact because they make you feel like you've done something wrong or that there's just something about you that makes it your responsibility that things aren't going well in your relationship. This blaming is followed by feelings of rage, pain, contempt, and shame.

ANXIETY IN RELATIONSHIP

Relationships may be challenging to navigate. Many obstacles must be overcome, but the most challenging is the "Shoulds," which are assumptions you have about your spouse, your relationship, or yourself. These assumptions bring a sense of entitlement, which is harmful to your relationship. It can even result in breakups.

It's a waste of time and energy to try to change your spouse into the person you want them to be. It will also result in frustration and disappointment. And the more upset you become, the more probable it is that you will do or say things that may harm your relationship.

Other individuals are beyond your control. Only you have power over yourself. So, the next time you feel compelled to control or modify someone else, consider whether it's essential. Is there any other option? Can you live with the situation as it is?

What part of the relationship do you play? Are you attempting to alter someone else's behavior? If that's the case, how's it going for you? Are you ready to accept full responsibility for all of your emotions and reactions?

Stop and ask yourself if what you're doing is helping or damaging your relationship the very next time you catch yourself worrying about "shoulds."

What Is The Concept Of "Shoulds"?

In a relationship, the notion of "shoulds" is the most difficult to express and often brings about misinterpreted ideas. "Shoulds" refer to the notion that you should act or feel a specific way because society, your parents, friends, or partners expect us to. The idea of "shoulds" may be a very harmful way to live, and it can damage our relationships in the end.

The truth is that no one should teach you how to feel or act in your relationship. You have the right to feel and behave whichever way you choose without feeling bad about it. Don't do anything if you don't want to do it!

The term "should" is deceptive. It could be used to persuade us to do something we don't want to do (or don't have time to do) or persuade somebody to act in a way we believe they should. "Should" is a prescriptive word. You've taken a value judgment on what you think is essential in life if you say, "I should be doing something." Here's when the difficulty begins. You may be condemning your spouse for failing to fulfill your standards, or you may be judging yourself for failing to meet your own. In either situation, you're upset and furious, and you're blaming it on somebody else.

Even long-term relationships may be sabotaged by the notion of "shoulds," which make you feel like you're not living up to others' or our own expectations of ourselves. When others or ourselves fail to satisfy those assumptions, we condemn them or ourselves, resulting in hatred. Resentment makes you angry, making it difficult to relate to people lovingly and compassionately.

You have the moral right to decide at any time. If you first agreed to go out to dinner with your partner but later decided that you could instead remain at home and watch a film, then stay at home! No one has the authority to make you feel like you're "abandoning" them if you cancel your plans at the last minute.

It's critical to realize that saying yes doesn't imply that you are obligated to perform anything you agreed to.

The Personal Responsibility Principle

"Shoulds" are harmful in a love connection. It's a significant red flag if one person feels like they're constantly supporting the relationship, or if one person feels as if they're continually providing while another is constantly receiving.

Love, in reality, is a give-and-take situation. Each individual in a partnership must be accountable for their joy. They must realize that it is not their partner's responsibility to make them happy; it is their responsibility.

While it's OK to love somebody and you would like to see them joyful, you wouldn't have the capacity to make your partner happy, nor do you have the authority to make them love you unconditionally. Your role is to respect yourself enough to not settle for much less than you deserve, and to express your needs clearly and frequently so that you may both obtain what you should get from the connection.

In a relationship, the notion of "should" is linked to the principle of personal responsibility. There are several compelling reasons why they occur:

Your Partner Is Too Dependent On You

A good relationship necessitates autonomy and independence. If your spouse can't make decisions without you, he isn't entirely in charge of his life, leading to future issues. In reality, both spouses benefit from having their own lives and hobbies outside of their partnership. It's a clear indicator of problems when one person feels overly reliant on the other.

To Handle Relationship Disagreements

A relationship is made up of two people who may differ on specific subjects from time to time. For instance, if you want to go on vacation but your partner prefers to stay at home, you both have options. If one of you is angry about your spouse's decision or attempts to persuade him to make a different one, that person feels he has the power to dominate and force his partner to do what he wants. This attitude is bad for the relationship since it breeds bitterness and hostility.

Pulling Your Relationship Out of a Rut

Couples frequently feel trapped in a rut and become disappointed when no progress is made. It is reasonable, but it might be an issue with their techniques rather than the relationship's strength. Strategies for satisfying your requirements are not like computer programs that you can simply type in and execute. They'll need to change as you learn more. Try a different method if your current one isn't working. But it won't work until you make a firm, deliberate choice to change your ways.

To Handle Conflicts

You'll create new and better strategies to achieve what you want if you grow excellent at handling conflicts in your relationship. As you learn to handle difficulties together, your problem-solving skills will adapt to your relationship's shifting conditions. For example, if one spouse is controlling and exacting, the other will need to devise different tactics to deal with this behavior.

Six Steps Of Personal Responsibility

The Six Steps of Personal Responsibility follow a relationship's natural growth. They're built on the idea that we all have choices in our lives and that if we make the appropriate ones, we can have healthy relationships.

The Six Actions of Personal Responsibility are six steps that one must take to be accountable for oneself, which leads to a higher feeling of responsibility in interpersonal relationships. These are the six steps of personal responsibility:

1. Accepting responsibility is the first step. "What am I willing to alter, or how can I improve it?" you must ask yourself. You must be willing to adjust your reaction if you want to stop your partner from shouting at you. Consider the

scenario from your partner's point of view and consider what you could do better.

2. The second stage is to have a conversation with your partner about how you both want your relationship to develop. What are your requirements? What are some factors that may benefit or harm the relationship?

3. The third step is to schedule a time when you and your partner can talk about what you both believe should happen in your relationship. Ensure that everyone has a chance to express their thoughts. Discuss the issues arising and what each individual requires to keep the relationship continuing.

4. Compromise is the fourth phase. A healthy relationship requires reaching a consensus on solutions that satisfies all parties involved. It entails communicating openly and honestly with one another so that no one feels left out or disregarded. It consists of listening with as little judgment as possible, and then devising a strategy that will benefit everybody.

5. The ability to forgive and forget is the fifth stage. We learn tolerance as children, and we often forget it as adults. When things go wrong,

forgiveness frees you to try again without the burden of the past.

6. Forgive your spouse if they make a mistake. It is perhaps the most difficult of all the steps, since you must let go of your bitterness toward them for their faults.

7. Last but not least, personal responsibility boils down to being truthful in a partnership. You'll feel much better if you really can be honest with yourself and look at issues honestly. Your partner may not want to know that this is over and that you're not the one for them, but you'll feel good when you can be truthful with yourself and look at issues objectively. If you're dissatisfied with your relationship, don't stay solely to avoid change. Whenever it's time to move on, make the necessary adjustments.

Lying is a type of deception that may ruin a relationship; it's critical to be honest with yourself about whatever you want in a relationship, and continuously recognize when it's necessary to leave.

CHAPTER 11: TIME-OUTS

Partners can benefit from using Time-Out. This little break might assist you in reconnecting with your mate and repairing your connection.

The term "needing a time-out" might indicate different things to various people. The most commonly used word is a break taken by one or both partners of a relationship. This might be a prolonged period with no communication.

A time-out should be agreed upon when both parties are calm and uninfluenced by anger or dissatisfaction. Determine how much time is required to achieve the objective ahead of time, and take actions to guarantee that any side can achieve the goal within that timeframe. Doing so will avoid placing undue strain on your relationship or yourself by having unreasonable expectations.

If your partner is unwilling to participate in a time-out with you, try obtaining aid from friends or family or even a professional counselor. If your partner refuses, the relationship may be irreparable. Even if you're able to sort things out together, keep in mind that going through these types of circumstances too soon can cause a lot of stress.

Ignoring tension can be visible and unpleasant, leading to relationship problems. However, taking a break from your relationship might be beneficial. Both parties have the opportunity to calm down and collect their ideas to talk appropriately, without inflicting more harm to the relationship.

When partners have trouble resolving their disagreements, they use a relationship time-out. Even if two people like one other and want to be together, they aren't always compatible. They may be arguing too much, or they may simply be growing apart. Whatever the cause, they need to spend some time apart from each other to find out what is wrong and how to best address it.

If you think you might need a time-out, here are some tips to help you make the most of it:

1. Determine a "we need a break" signal which is either vocal or nonverbal. Make your verbal agreement as brief as possible, such as "Time-out" or "Break!". This agreement should never be expressed in a combative tone. You can create a T with your hands or make a peace sign to utilize a nonverbal sign. Discuss your options with your partner and figure out what works best for both of you.
2. Agree on what constitutes nasty arguing. Nasty arguing can include name-calling, harsh words, or raised voices for most couples.
3. Discuss the purpose of a break. A time-out is ideal for avoidant people. However, more needy spouses may interpret this as an indication that their partner doesn't care about them. It's important to talk about what a break means to you both.

4. Organize how you will spend your break. Your capacity to relax is determined by what you think and do during your break. You must make a deliberate effort to replace tough ideas with relationship-enhancing ones that will calm you down in order for a break to be helpful.
5. Reconnect with each other again. Don't leap right back into the fight when you return from your break. Instead, concentrate on rekindling emotional connections with one another. You're telling your brain that your mate is someone you can trust by reconnecting.

Determine The Cause For Your Need For A Time-Out

A cause for requiring a time-out may be evident at times, but it may take some self-reflection to determine what is truly upsetting you about your spouse or your relationship. Identifying the cause for your need for a time-out can make it simpler to come up with answers to any problems in your relationship.

Ensure you and your partner are on the same page about what constitutes a time-out. All parties must be aware of how long the time-out will continue. If one party believes it will persist until they have a chat while the other believes it is more of an endless delay, the context of the conversation might quickly devolve into a power struggle.

Theoretical Background

It is critical to realize that conflict increases faster than it deescalates in partnerships. There are at least two sequences of disagreeable actions in the typical relationship. Patterson (1982) investigated how anger rises.

He discovered that couples engage in a series of despicable acts to affect or dominate the other person. The first sequence generally consists of one person making demands and threatening another.

The second phase is performed by the person who is the target of the demands and threats. The recipient's answer might be interpreted as an attempt to mend the relationship or as an attempt to get revenge in some manner for being intimidated or forced upon.

A third sequence begins in which the pair returns to their contact before the first threat. In other words, an interaction requires at least three exchanges before it can be called complete.

An instant time-out is the only way to break a pattern of assault and counter-attack. The individual must walk out of the room to calm down. The other immediately follows when one spouse leaves the room, exacerbating the emotional cycle. After you've given yourself a break and achieved some dynamic space, you may resume issue-solving and communication.

The first time-out may appear to the partner as a punishment since they disrupt whatever conduct they were involved in at the time. Your goal, however, is not punishment, but rather the disruption of a well-rehearsed response pattern. The objective is not just to modify their attitude, but also to break the way that leads to aggravation.

Aversive chains are harmful interactions between people that start with one person's unpleasant conduct and progress into a sequence of increasingly terrible behaviors by both parties. A time-out stops the escalation and allows both parties to settle down and consider things through.

If you're in an escalating disagreement with your partner, the first thing you should do is acknowledge that an unpleasant chain is in motion. It helps to give it a name: "Okay, we're going to start an unpleasant chain." If you spot it early on, it will be a lot easier to stop than if you wait until after the pattern has acquired momentum.

When you identify that the pattern has begun, you must interrupt it using a time-out. This causes a momentary gap in the rhythm, giving both participants time to relax.

History

The "time-out" process is a fundamental procedure that may be traced back to Daniel Sonkin and Dr. Jeanie Deschner (Sonkin and Durphy 1985; Deschner 1984). The time-out is a proactive method of breaking the cycle of rising anger, which can escalate into physical violence. It may also be utilized as a de-escalation interval when children are involved in a fight.

A time-out is a behavior modification strategy used to interrupt a bad behavior and calm both parties down. A time-out can also regain emotional control, therefore reducing disruptive behavior.

Psychotherapist Charles Ferster (1962) invented the term "time-out" after discovering that placing a child in an empty room for 20 seconds with no verbal or physical contact might interrupt a tantrum. Daniel Sonkin later modified the approach for use in marital disputes.

Time-outs are a simple and successful method for averting many occurrences of domestic violence. Although they were created to control children's misbehavior, they may be tailored to fit the needs of spouses who want to restore love and peace to their relationships.

Time-outs are not a fast answer for significant issues. They are intended to teach individuals how to quit being angry and calm down in order to discuss their disagreements without being aggressive or defensive. Time-outs, like any talent, require practice. They will not work if the pair does not adhere to the time-out agreement.

The duration might range from a few minutes to several hours. Time-outs should be long enough for each individual to connect with their feelings and work out how to solve the situation, without using anger or violence.

Agree On A Timeout Signal

Agreeing on a unique time-out signal might help you resolve conflicts quickly and avoid significant battles in your relationship.

When things start to grow hot in the present, a time-out signal is a notion for actively taking a break or regrouping. It's a way to take a breather and express what some folks may already be experiencing.

Time-outs are an effective and valuable strategy for helping to diffuse or end a dispute. The time-out signal might assist each participant in relaxing and being conscious of their role in the disagreement.

In a relationship, agree on a time-out signal that either partner may utilize if they need to step back and relax.

The signal should be something that the other partner notices, but not anything that will cause a public uproar (e.g., hanging a sock on the door handle).

The goal is to allow oneself time and space to relax. Some individuals prefer to go somewhere quiet, such as their bedroom or another room in the house, whereas others prefer to go out for some fresh air.

You can agree that that the time-out will end after a certain amount of time or when one person returns and asks the other for forgiveness for whatever has offended them.

When you're furious with your partner, a timeout might be reasonable, but don't use it to unload your wrath on them - for example, "I'm going for a time-out, so you'd best listen to what I have to say." It may also assist if both spouses agree not to bring up new disagreements during a time-out — instead, use the opportunity to reflect on an earlier-in-the-day fight.

When one becomes agitated, you may utilize the time-out process to prevent things from growing into a full-fledged disagreement. If your spouse begins to lash out, you must intervene before things get out of hand. The most basic technique is to utilize the "T" symbol, which is used in basketball and other sports. You don't have to say anything. When things get heated, you make the "T" gesture, and your spouse either reciprocates or says, "OK, time-out."

You then excuse yourself for a minute or two and go for a stroll or take some deep breaths. This gives you both a chance to relax, so you may chat about whatever is bugging you.

The most crucial aspect of implementing time-outs is that they only function if both spouses agree and are prepared to follow through. The rule is null and void when one person does it and the other does not reciprocate in kind. Don't be shocked if your spouse first refuses to accept your time-out requests.

The Early Warning Signal

Everyone experiences the same early warning indicators of increasing rage. If you're having problems recognizing them in yourself, ask friends and family to alert you when they notice your anger rising.

A variety of circumstances might contribute to the escalation of rage. One characteristic in common is a sensation of being personally assaulted, even when this is not the case. Name-calling, finger-pointing, humiliating, accusing, threatening, or any kind of violent behavior should result in an instant time-out.

Another significant component is any remark that begins with "you," even if it is favorable; phrases like, "You never..." or, "You always..." are seen as an attack on the partner's character by the partner. Furthermore, when you use the term "always," you make a misleading generalization about your spouse's past and present conduct. This might be offensive and cause hate in your relationship.

Use the term "never" with utmost caution - for example, never remark, "You never assist around the home!" Instead, say something like, "I noticed you didn't help me around the home the other day."

The abrupt introduction of a sensitive issue in a quarrel is an early warning sign that your relationship is in peril. You're talking about auto repairs when the topic abruptly shifts to one of your partner's spending habits. When a painful thing is thrown into a confrontation, the focus includes prior crimes and infractions.

People bring up sensitive topics during arguments for a variety of reasons. Someone may be attempting to shift attention away from the issue at hand, or they may be feeling uneasy about their actions and wishing to put the other person on the defensive. Time-outs, for whatever cause, might be an early warning indication that your relationship is experiencing an upsurge in conflict.

Quit speaking for a moment if you find yourself in a time-out during a fight. If you can't stop talking, respectfully disagree on this topic for the time being and set another time to discuss it later.

Make Rules For Time-Outs

You have the authority to establish time-out rules in your relationship. This is the time to de-escalate and potentially even resolve conflicts together. You have control throughout the time-out - who receives one, and what is anticipated during the time-out.

These are some of the rules for time-outs in a relationship:

Possible Time-Out Locations

The best spot for a time-out is somewhere peaceful, away from any distractions and disruptions. You have the option of using a bedroom or another private place.

What You Should Expect During Time-Outs

You can expect the individual given the time-out to stay silent and composed during the time-out. It is not permissible for them to get noisy or hurl insults during a time-out. A time-out is intended to assist both parties in calming down, and perhaps come up with solutions to difficulties.

Move On From The Forum Wars

They are not a forum for debate. There are no speeches, final words, or explanations. This may appear harsh, but it is the only way to prevent the dreaded circular discussions, which generally result in even more hurt and rage.

A Time-Out Chair

No returning to the subject matter until both parties have calmed down. Because you don't know how long you'll be in the time-out chair, plan ahead of time what you'll do to keep yourself occupied during this period of forced solitude. Read a book or solve a puzzle, meditate or envision a serene location, listen to music—do whatever works best for you.

Truth About Time-Out

Don't say anything about what occurred during the argument. Do not whine about being sent in time-out or what happened during the disagreement.

A Time-Out Clock

Set a 10-minute timer. When one person requests a time-out, the other person sets a clock for ten minutes and walks to the chosen location alone to wait out the time-out period without disruptions from their partner. After 10 minutes, they should return and talk about whatever they want to express without being interrupted until they are through.

Practice The Time-Outs

Your well-being means you must practice time-outs in a relationship. If you are going through a challenging period and cannot address a problem with your spouse, taking some "me" time might help you recover. It will also allow you to clear your beliefs in your own minds.

Are you attempting to empty your mind? Choose a time-out location and go there. This may be a coffee shop or a park seat where you know you won't be disturbed by others. Carry a magazine or newspaper to enjoy, or a diary and pen to record your thoughts during your time away.

When you cannot leave home due to injury or disease, set aside a room as your time-out zone, close yourself off from the outer world for a while, and reflect on what is bugging you about your relationship. Call a buddy for help if feasible, but don't tell anybody else about this activity — you want complete privacy during this downtime.

Trying to resolve disagreements as soon as possible might lead to rash judgments or statements that you may come to regret later. Taking a break frequently allows you to reflect on the issue before saying something that may irritate the other person or increase your emotions.

Time-outs are advised in every relationship when there is a possibility of disagreement. Ties such as romantic ones, parent-child connections, sibling relationships, and even friendships fall under this category. The procedure is straightforward: one person quits speaking while the other turns away or waits in another place until they feel relaxed enough to resume chatting. It makes no difference who initiates the time-out initially, as long as both persons are willing to participate.

The principles for using time-outs in a relationship are straightforward:

1. The individual requesting the time-out must state their request correctly.
2. The other person must agree to it, and then both parties must act on it.
3. The individual requesting the time-out must be willing to make an apparent vow about when to return, talk again, and then keep that pledge.
4. If something comes up during the time-out that causes you not to meet your commitment, you must promptly notify the other person and reschedule or renegotiate the time-out.

CHAPTER 12: THE ROLE OF EMOTIONAL INTELLIGENCE

Emotional intelligence is an essential component of every relationship, and if one of the partners lacks it, it will be challenging for them to live peacefully with the other. The fundamental function of emotional intelligence in a relationship allows couples to communicate and understand one another without difficulties. This trait also aids them in overcoming any difficulties in their path, and because they can deal with any problem with ease, they may live calmly and joyfully.

This attribute is critical since every human being has emotions and sentiments. Individuals lose their sense of identity and get isolated from the rest of the world when they don't share their feelings due to fear or doubts.

Emotional intelligence enables you to convey your sentiments to individuals who matter the most to you, which means that both sides will feel more at ease discussing their difficulties rather than keeping them bottled up inside.

You can comprehend your partner's feelings without being informed how they feel if you have high emotional intelligence. You can sense if they are pleased or unhappy without saying anything, and you may utilize this information to help them feel better.

Your emotional intelligence is crucial in your relationships; from the person you date to your friends. Emotional intelligence can help you connect more effectively at work and play.

Emotional intelligence does not imply always being polite or friendly, but it does mean recognizing when you're acting poorly and making no efforts to correct that behavior. It entails comprehending why you feel the way you do, and constructively articulating your emotions.

People with poor emotional intelligence frequently suffer in relationships because they don't comprehend what makes them happy or unhappy or how they appear to others. They could be quick to rage or strike out at others around them without understanding why, and they may fail to consider how their actions will affect those around them.

The Impact Of The Lack Of Emotional Intelligence

Emotional intelligence is the capacity to recognize, appraise, and manage one's own, other people's, and a group's emotions. It is a talent that directly influences our performance in every relationship or organization. It is crucial in all aspects of our life, including our connections with family members, friends, spouses, and coworkers.

Emotionally intelligent couples are more empathetic and caring toward each other. Emotionally brilliant partners can talk honestly and openly with one another and healthily process their emotions. They can handle problems peacefully rather than let them escalate into something more serious. These couples also have more trust and intimacy than less emotionally intelligent couples.

It is difficult to break old patterns, but learning to be honest and open with your partner will help you have a good marriage.

Here are a few examples of how emotional intelligence may help a relationship:

Recognize Your Partner's Emotions

Listening to their partner's feelings is one approach for couples to understand one another better. When people express their emotions to their spouses, they must listen closely and reflect on what they heard. It will allow them to comprehend their partner's emotions better and understand how they see the world around them.

Use Your Emotions Appropriately

People must know when they are sad or angry so they. can channel their emotions instead of suppressing them. If someone is depressed, they should strive to put themselves in a position to feel good. Similarly, if someone is upset or disappointed, they should spend some time alone to cool down before interacting with their partner or loved ones again.

Handling Your Emotions

Emotional intelligence is defined by the ability to control one's emotions. Adding another person to the mix adds a whole new level of emotion to the scene. Emotions get more intense as you get older, and the degree changes depending on who you're with.

Allowing oneself to feel your thoughts without judgment and then using them as a source of knowledge to decide things is what emotional intelligence includes. It does not imply dismissing or disregarding your sentiments; rather, it entails looking at them objectively, and then moving ahead based on what you learn from that process.

Here are some pointers to help you better manage your emotions and how they impact your relationship:

Handle Your Own Emotions First

It's simple for one individual to criticize the other for their difficulties, especially if they lack emotional management skills. You may modify this by accepting responsibility for your own emotions rather than blaming others. If someone else irritates you, take a step back and consider whether you contributed to the situation as well. You may discover that while both of you are to blame for creating a problematic situation, neither of you accepts responsibility for how you feel about it. Use your emotions as a guide when confronted with a circumstance that bothers or frustrates you.

Be Mindful Of The Reasons Behind Your Feelings

Understanding why you are angry or disturbed may help you manage these emotions better. For example, consider discussing the matter with your spouse to find a solution if she mistreats you.

However, if you feel ignored by your partner, remember that individuals need time and space to satisfy their needs, which does not always imply that they no longer love you.

Accept Responsibility For Your Emotions

It's simple to blame other people for how you feel, but doing so will increase tension and make it more difficult for the two of you to work through these emotions together.

Recognize The Distinction Between Being Bothered And Being Furious

Feeling irritated is a natural aspect of every relationship; however, becoming enraged over minor matters might be a symptom of deeper troubles inside the partnership.

Acquire Emotional Intelligence

The study of Emotional Intelligence (EQ) has grown in prominence over the last decade as people have become more conscious of its significance. The rationale is straightforward: EQ is critical to relationship success.

To have a good, happy connection with someone else, you must read and comprehend their feelings and thoughts. Because we are all emotional beings, we must understand how to manage our own emotions and interpret the feelings of our partners. Emotional Intelligence is the capacity to perceive, appraise, and manage one's own emotions as well as those of others.

Many individuals underestimate the importance of emotional intelligence in a relationship. If a person lacks EQ, they do not understand how to manage their negative feelings, which can cause difficulties for themselves and their relationship.

So, how does this look? Here are a few relational examples of emotional intelligence:

- They can detect when somebody is upset or wounded without responding or lashing out at their partner.
- They are aware of their flaws and talents and may modify their actions accordingly.
- They understand when to seek assistance and when to manage situations independently.
- When dealing with problems, they understand how to balance listening and speaking.

Achieve emotional intelligence in several ways, including:

Recognize Your Emotions

It would be best to recognize the emotions you are experiencing at any particular time. You should determine if you are angry, sad, or nervous.

Investigate Your Feeling

Once you've determined what emotion you're experiencing, investigate why you're experiencing it. Be truthful with yourself about why you feel the way you do. Instead of dismissing or ignoring your emotions, strive to understand them so that you may take control of them rather than allowing them to dominate you.

Translate Your Feelings into Words

What does it mean to be sad, angry, annoyed, or disappointed? Emotions become less abstract and more straightforward to grasp when defined in this manner, both for yourself and for others.

Manage Your Negative Emotions

Rather than eliminating unpleasant feelings, understanding how to manage them is the most excellent approach to start conquering them.

Practice Empathy

Have you ever been in a relationship where your spouse is constantly unhappy, constantly shouting, and continually blaming you for their sadness? Or have you ever been on the receiving end of this in a relationship? It may be a nightmare in any case.

People with low emotional maturity are notorious for criticizing others for their issues. They are oblivious to their involvement in what is going wrong in a relationship.

These folks have no idea how to apologize, since they believe the fault is due to someone else. They have no idea how to make people happy because they think happiness originates somewhere else. They don't know how to follow through since they believe others should do it for them. And they are oblivious to being misled by others, because they believe deception is something that only other individuals do to them.

If you're dating someone with poor emotional intelligence, you might be in for a long and challenging journey. It's challenging to be around folks who blame everyone except themselves for their dissatisfaction. The great news is that if you start showing empathy to your partner, your relationship will improve dramatically.

What is the definition of empathy? Simply described, it is the ability to empathize with the experiences of others by seeing oneself in their shoes. In other words, empathy enables you to comprehend where another person is coming from, why they feel or think the way they do, and what they may be feeling emotionally. Empathy also assists you in seeing that everyone has difficulties and challenges.

A shared sense of empathy characterizes the most exemplary partnerships. It feels comfortable and secure to be in a relationship with someone who knows and cares about your feelings. However, if your partner isn't sympathetic to your feelings, it might be tough to form a trustworthy relationship.

Empathy is a crucial component of every strong relationship because it fosters trust, strengthens relationships, and creates harmony between two individuals who genuinely care about one other. Indeed, many psychologists believe empathy to be one of the most important aspects of love and necessary for maintaining a good relationship over time. The greater your ability to empathize with your partner's emotions, the stronger your bond will be.

Differentiate Sympathy From Empathy

Sympathy is the sharing of another person's burden. It's the "I feel your anguish" point of view.

When dealing with a close friend or family member who has had a crisis, expressing sympathy helps them know that you understand and care about their predicament. However, compassion may be harmful in an already troubled relationship, since it promotes the belief that one person is to blame for the other partner's troubles.

It's easy to slip into this trap when you're feeling sorry for yourself: "I'm so sorry for you that I'm prepared to let you take advantage of me."

On the other hand, empathy is a more nuanced emotion than pity. It does not imply that you are feeling someone else's grief; instead, it demands you to put yourself in their shoes and envision what they may be feeling and thinking.

Empathy entails being present for someone when they require it – listening when appropriate and assisting when needed. But compassion is not the same as sympathy. It does not require you to make justifications for someone else's bad behavior, or take accountability for the other person's situation. Empathy allows couples to work together to address difficulties, allowing each individual to accept responsibility for their own well-being.

The distinction between sympathy and empathy is that compassion feels sad for someone, but empathy is feeling. When someone has a difficulty or a tragedy, we should not feel sorry for them. Instead, we should strive to understand how our partner thinks in such a position, and assist them in resolving or coping with the difficulty or bad fortune in the best manner possible.

Empathy necessitates an accurate perception of another person's thoughts and feelings, which allows us to be delicate to their interests and needs, predict their reactions, and adequately adjust our behavior while considering our opinions, emotions, requirements, and preferences.

Self-Regulation And Emotional Intelligence

Telling your lover everything you dislike about them is counterproductive to the relationship. It's also not a good idea to be needy, clinging, demanding, or overbearing.

Self-regulation is an essential skill for couples to learn since it helps sustain harmony in a relationship and prevents both partners from acting excessively. It is vital, as it allows us to set healthy boundaries in relationships and moderate our emotions when things become too heated.

Partners who can manage their emotions will likely have more healthy relationships than those who cannot. Self-regulation refers to your ability to keep yourself in control when interacting with others and your reactions to them. When you overreact, you exacerbate rather than deescalate the problem. Maintaining self-control regardless of how you feel about someone else can help you retain peace in your relationship, even when things do not go your way.

Self-regulation tasks include the following:

- Maintaining a calendar and keeping scheduled meetings.
- Managing your emotions and resisting the need to strike out when angry or unhappy.
- Maintaining your focus on tasks for extended periods
- Keeping your expenditures under control.
- Make sure that you do assignments at work or school before the deadlines.

Comprehending that realizing somebody else's point of view does not need you to give up your point of view is the key to enhancing your emotional intelligence in partnerships. It may appear weird, yet it is correct. When you comprehend someone else's point of view, you shouldn't have to agree with them or embrace the conclusion they get from it.

When you lose sight of this when disputing with your spouse, you become irritated because you believe they are not listening to what you have to say. It leads to a dispute about who wasn't hearing initially, and maybe to an escalation of fury in which neither party is listening any longer.

The trick is to grasp what the other person is saying and why they feel that way, rather than simply listening. You can still have your viewpoint - their feelings are genuine even if yours aren't — but you can now listen without attempting to alter their mind or becoming upset.

The following duties are part of emotional intelligence in a relationship:

- To comprehend, embrace, and be conscious of your sensations and emotions.
- To comprehend other people's sentiments and emotions and accept them for what they are, but not be caught in by them.
- To comprehend what is going on in a relationship between you and another person.
- Managing your sensations, emotions, and their expression.

Handling Your Partner's Emotions

The partnership is not a rivalry. When one spouse begins to feel competitive, they will start to view their partner's activities unfavorably and as a direct danger to their relationship's success. This competition will produce conflict since the competitive partner will lose the other partner.

No matter how much you love and care for your mate, there may be times when they hurt your feelings. Understanding how to deal with such feelings might help you get past the pain and strengthen your relationship.

The first step in dealing with your partner's feelings in a relationship is your tone. Your tone is fundamental in your relationships, and this is something you must both focus on together. If one person's manner is cruel and judgmental while the other's tone is bright, optimistic, and playful, neither of you will be capable of handling one another's emotions healthily.

Understanding where your partner's emotions are coming from is the second step in dealing with them in a relationship. We all have varied experiences that form our worldview, including our relationships. Whenever anyone says or does anything that offends us, we should inquire why they said or did it. In many situations, their aim is not to injure you but rather to harm themselves and strike. Still, you should always know that no matter what occurs between you, you must always say beautiful things about them behind their backs and in front of their faces because they deserve it.

CHAPTER 13: SELF-DISCLOSURE AND TRUST

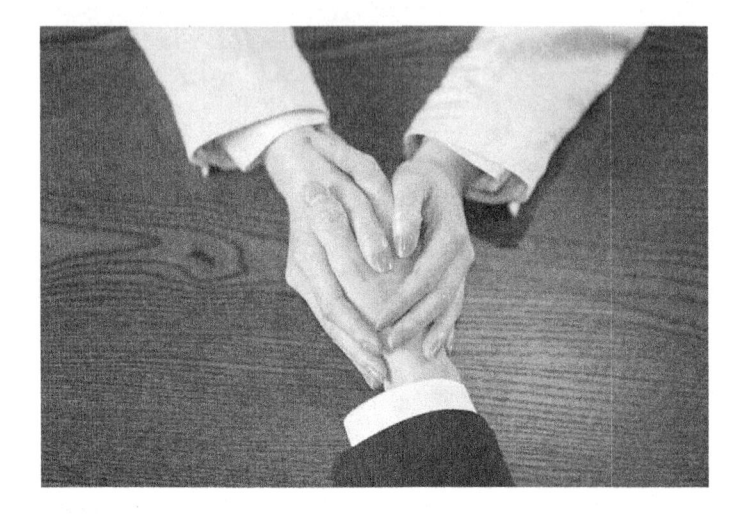

Many relationship specialists have investigated how self-disclosure influences trust in a partnership.

The explanation is that self-disclosure may harm or assist a relationship's trust component. Self-disclosure is the act of being honest and open with your spouse

It entails disclosing personal details, ideas, and emotions to the individual you are dating. The purpose of self-disclosure is to establish an intimate connection with your spouse so that you may learn about one another, identify common ground, and build a more incredible feeling of trust. However, if done poorly, you may wind up damaging your relationship.

Having the correct balance in your relationship is essential for successful self-disclosure. Too much self-disclosure might make you appear needy, nervous, and anxious for your spouse's approval. Suppose there is insufficient self-disclosure in a relationship. In that case, it can lead to fatigue and isolation, which will ultimately ruin any hope of an excellent long-term connection with your partner.

How do you strike the proper balance? The trick is to know how much disclosure is too much, and what style performs better based on the timeline of your relationship.

Be Open Mutually

Few people are at ease discussing the bad parts of their lives. Some persons may have suffered from sadness, anxiety, or disease. Others may have experienced the termination of a relationship or the loss of a career. It is critical to have open communication with your partner, regardless of the circumstances.

If you're unsure whether or not to tell your partner something, consider if you would want them to tell you if they were in your position. If the answer is yes, you should likely inform them; if the response is no, you should consider avoiding bringing it up.

Keep in mind that even if you tell your partner about something, they are under no obligation to accept or believe it. It is natural for anyone to seek proof or credible evidence when coping with something they've never dealt with before. It might be a physical condition, such as a sickness or problem, a psychological feature, such as nervousness, or anything else related to you as an individual. However, if you give evidence to them (for example, by providing previous medical documents), they may be more willing to accept what you say.

Develop Your Relationship

The act of disclosing personal information about oneself to others is known as self-disclosure. It is a communication style that can aid in the strengthening of interpersonal connections and the feeling of being more connected to people.

Self-disclosure is one technique to become more personal with someone through conversation by providing details about yourself that would not come up in the usual course of ordinary chitchat. It may also be used to show others that you care about them and are at ease around them, leading to higher trust and stronger connections.

Telling somebody something intimate about yourself is an act of trust; therefore, creating a connection with self-disclosure necessitates the development of a trusting relationship.

Like other parts of your relationships, self-disclosure requires a certain amount of give and take. When you are willing to share secret or privileged information, you care about others. In turn, receiving information from another person through personal disclosures or insights into who they are, and what they think or feel demonstrates that they are ready to share anything about themselves with you. Self-disclosure creates emotional bonds, because it brings people together on a personal level.

Accept Each Other's Past

Attempting to modify your partner's history will result in an unhappy pair and may lead to the end of your relationship.

Attempting to alter the past means asking your spouse to change who they have been, whatever they have done, or where they have been. That individual is powerless to change their history. Your spouse may have regretted prior behaviors, but those acts were performed and cannot be altered. You can pardon your spouse for previous behaviors, but you also can't expect them to act differently in the future than they have in the past.

When partners strive to modify one another's pasts, they end up feeling as if they have lost themselves in their relationship. They frequently feel powerless, discouraged, and resentful of their relationship. Neither of these emotions is favorable for improving or maintaining your relationship.

Accepting one another's history, according to Masini, can be challenging at the most difficult periods in a relationship. Both parties, however, must recognize that the other has improved since the heinous behavior or error. She advised you to accept your mate. If you expect perfection from your significant other, you will be dissatisfied with the outcome.

Be The Source Of Confidence

A woman may express a desire for a man who is more "assuring," but what she truly means is that he must be her source of confidence.

Here are five strategies to become the source of trust in a relationship:

1. Be a part of the same team. Being on the same team implies that you and your spouse share similar goals for your relationship and your life. You're both striving toward comparable objectives, and you're supportive of one another.
2. Be open and honest with one another. If anything is upsetting you, talk about it with your partner rather than keeping it to yourself. It is advisable to discuss problems immediately, rather than wait to evolve into more serious problems later.
3. Show your spouse that you care about their feelings by being sympathetic and avoiding pointing out their defects or shortcomings.

4. Have enough faith in one another to do what is best, rather than making selfish decisions that benefit only yourself.
5. Talk about your previous relationships. Suppose previous relationships left wounded sentiments or emotional damage. In that case, both parties must communicate about those feelings and focus on healing them and also resolving any problems that may have contributed to the split in the first place. Talking about these things honestly can help you get past them and tackle any underlying issues or worries, so they don't become roadblocks later.

The Effect Of Different Factors On The Extent Of Self-Disclosure

In a relationship, self-disclosure is a component that might impact the connection. When someone is open about themselves, they might want to become closer to you or maybe they are at ease with you. When there is little self-disclosure, it might be because they are not happy with you or do not want to become closer to you.

In a relationship, the amount of self-disclosure is significant for both parties. To build feelings of connection and to belong with their partner, one spouse must have a high level of self-disclosure. If one person does not want their partner to feel too close to them or is unwilling to build a tighter relationship, it is also critical for one partner to be a low self-discloser.

Each individual in the relationship must be aware of self-disclosure and its impact on the relationship. It is also essential for each individual in the relationship to know how their amount of self-disclosure affects both their spouse and them. When a person reveals too much about themselves, their spouse may get uneasy.

Various aspects contribute to self-disclosure in a relationship. These criteria include the quantity of time spent with one's spouse and the length of time they have been together. The amount of time spent with someone influences how much information they feel comfortable disclosing about themselves. Furthermore, the amount of time two individuals have known each other also influences how much self-disclosure happens in a relationship.

Tension also influences self-disclosure and how much you share with others. When stress rises, so does the level of self-disclosure in a connection. Furthermore, when there is an imbalance between couples, there is more self-disclosure and there are more preconceptions, such as women being more prone than males to disclosing sentiments.

How Does Self-Disclosure Bridge The Gap?

It is advantageous to employ self-disclosure to bridge the gap in a relationship, since it allows individuals to be entirely honest with one another. It also acts as an icebreaker and helps people learn more about one another. Self-disclosure may be employed in job interviews, dating relationships, friendships, and even casual social encounters with strangers.

The act of providing personal information about oneself is known as self-disclosure. Sharing individual facts about your life with others aids in the development of lasting connections by exposing them to new facets of your personality. Religion, opinions, ideas, sentiments, and even family history can all be considered personal information.

The advantages of self-disclosure are numerous, and it aids in developing interpersonal connections. Self-disclosure, for example, improves closeness and offers a sense of comfort between two individuals who share personal views. Someone feels more at ease with people they know well, making self-disclosure a powerful way to connect two people. Self-disclosure can also encourage people to open up to you, resulting in a stronger relationship.

One of the simplest methods to develop a self-disclosure connection is sending "I" communications. These are sentences that start with "I" and are about how you feel, such as, "I get annoyed when I'm among individuals who don't know how to communicate their sentiments." When you express your sentiments to another person in this manner, they will be more ready to open up and disclose personal information to you.

CHAPTER 14: NON-VERBAL COMMUNICATION

What Is Non-Verbal Communication?

Non-verbal communication is how we express ourselves without words. Often this is through our facial expressions, posture, and physical gestures. For example, imagine talking to a person about an upcoming vacation. You may mention that your flight is two hours long using verb tense, but this does not convey emotions. On the other hand, it is much easier for the other person to understand what you mean if you show excitement and joy with facial expressions and gestures.

We don't know how someone else feels until they tell us; thus, nonverbal expressions are more significant than what we say. Their words may indicate one thing, but their body language conveys a completely another narrative.

Non-verbal communication is there to complement verbal communication. It's more of a way to show someone that you're interested in what they say. That is because this type of communication tends to make people uncomfortable. When you raise your eyebrows, for instance, or nod your head when someone else is talking, it shows them that you have an open mind and are willing to listen.

You'll also find that non-verbal communication is a lot more subtle than verbal communication. If you ask your partner how they feel about something and they say everything's fine - but they bite their nails while they're doing it - then you'll know something's wrong, and maybe it's not as good as they make it seem to be.

You can tell when you're getting into an argument with someone by the way they stand up and walk around the room, or even leave the room completely. You can tell if you're making progress in your relationship by the way he holds you or touches you - you might even notice it by his gaze or smile.

Many people will say that there's a big difference between verbal and non-verbal communication in relationships, but I'm going to go ahead and disagree with you on that one. Sure, verbal communication is a big part of our relationships, so we're not saying that doesn't play a role at all. But the reality is that non-verbal communication will make up a much larger part of our relationships. I'd say it's probably even more important.

Imagine someone being honest with this person by saying, "Hey, I'm sorry I was late. I lost my keys. I thought you were going to wait for me, but I got here as soon as I could." As you can see, many little things could go into that sentence. For example, why did they think the person would wait for them? Did they ever call or text and tell the person they wouldn't be there? Did they even try calling the person? They might have said, "I lost my keys," which implies that they left the keys somewhere, yet there was no word about it until now.

Then again, someone could say, "Hey, I'm sorry I'm late. My dog ate my keys." That would be a different situation entirely, in my opinion.

The Effect Of Non-Verbal Communication On Couple's Psychology

Whether we admit it or not, non-verbal communication impacts our relationships. Your non-verbal communication gives a better indication of how you're feeling than how you say something. If a boyfriend or girlfriend says they're fine, but their body language tells them otherwise, it's probably more helpful to pay attention to that than to whatever they just said.

Some effects of non-verbal communication on couple's psychology are below:

- Non-verbal communication, which can be facial expressions, has been one of the most important facets of human relationships. It conveys the individual's subjective emotions, which lead to unconscious thoughts and behaviors. In a relationship, there are times when partners may have different perceptions of the same situation, as it can be difficult to express one's feelings verbally. Non-verbal communication allows individuals to express a whole range of emotions without words.

- Also, non-verbal communication is important in identifying true feelings and intentions. There are many instances where words may not convey one's inner feelings and intentions in a relationship, hence body language takes over as an alternative way of communicating them. Non-verbal communication channels individuals' wishes and needs in a relationship. It also helps resolve conflicts by allowing individuals to voice their opinions and emotions when words are insufficient. Non-verbal communication is crucial in the relationship, as it facilitates and helps harmonize the couple's relationship.
- Many people use non-verbal communication on a day-to-day basis. If you are not communicating verbally with your partner, you could be missing some important information about them. For example, if someone is constantly yawning, they may be bored of the conversation or are possibly tired. It could result in an argument down the line, because one will think their needs are being met while the other will feel neglected and ignored.

- Focusing on non-verbal communication within your relationship will improve your overall communication skills and understanding of each other, leading to a happier relationship for all involved.
- Non-verbal communication helps us build up the necessary foundations for a healthy relationship. Emotional and non-verbal communication is a window to their thoughts and feelings for each individual. If you can see through this window, you can learn the other person's thoughts and feelings. You can understand their needs and wants.
- The way we communicate with others is one of the most important aspects of the relationship. Non-verbal communication is especially important in relationships because it gives us an insight into our partner's personality and why they act as they do, and allows us to get valuable insight into their innermost thoughts. It allows us to understand our partners better and see things from their point of view.

What Can You Do?

Steady Eye Contact

Eye contact is a powerful communication tool and often the one non-verbal signal in the human body that is understood across all languages, cultures, and age groups. Making good eye contact with people shows them that you are paying attention to them. They feel more comfortable in conversation with you and feel important to you. Eye contact is so powerful that when a person avoids eye contact with another person who has just told them something positive or negative about themselves, this signals another person's immediate negative reaction.

Showing Emotion And Care

Showing emotion in your face and body language is a gentler, more caring way of communicating with others. It is part of your conversation to show this directly – smile and use facial expressions to show emotions (happy, sad, or angry). Also, keep your arms open when someone wants to approach you, and lean slightly forward (not a threatening forward but just slightly) when they do.

Keep The Focus On Your Partner While Talking

To show someone that you are interested in them, you must maintain eye contact while they are speaking. It will help them feel comfortable and open to sharing more with you. You can also pepper your conversation with questions. Like, "And what did you think of that?" or, "Have you had any positive experiences like that before?" It is important to listen carefully and hear what the other person is saying to get the most out of your conversation.

Touch And Its Emotional Impact On Relieving Anxiety In A Relationship

Touch is important in all relationships, but especially important in developing relationships. Humans use touch to show love and affection for each other, whether between parent and child or between lovers or close friends. The problem is that humans have only two hands, so a good way to express affection would be to hug or kiss. It does not give the other person much choice and can be uncomfortable for both parties. After a while, people in a relationship will often hold back their touch out of fear that they are being too overaffectionate. But the truth is that none of this affects how they feel about each other. The only thing is that touching transfers energy between two people and to the person whose body is touched. The more you touch someone, the more you express your love for them, and the less uncomfortable they feel around you.

Do Some Chores, Like Cooking Or Cleaning, For Your Partner

Couples who share the chores and the responsibility of keeping up with the housework tend to have happier, more satisfying relationships. They also sometimes report that they feel good about themselves once a chore is over, since they did something for their partner. It is also a good way to make your partner happy, which will make you happy because you know they are happy.

Improving Non-Verbal Communication

There is no single greatest strategy to improve nonverbal communication, but a few strategies can sometimes help us better our relationships and behaviors. The tips and steps below will guide you through what needs improvement in your non-verbal communication habits:

Self-Awareness

Throughout life, we develop our non-verbal communication habits. The more we observe ourselves, notice and accept our flaws, the more we improve our non-verbal communication skills.

Try To Immerse Yourself In A New Culture

Secondly, to improve your non-verbal communication, you need to know the most practical way to improve it. If you are looking for an easy way to improve your non-verbal communication, try immersing yourself in a new culture. You can do this by traveling abroad or watching videos of unfamiliar cultures. Doing so will expose you to new ways of communicating that you can then adopt into your own behavior.

Refine Your Non-Verbal Communication

The most important aspect of non-verbal communication is being conscious of it. Think about how you're communicating and be aware of your signals to other people. Work on refining your non-verbal communication, and you will be better equipped to get what you want out of every interaction with others.

Body Language Should Be Affirmative

Lastly, the most important aspect of improving non-verbal communication is watching how people respond to you by observing them and their body language. This tip also tells you to choose your words in order to respond positively to people.

How Does It Treat Anxiety And Mistrust?

Non-verbal communication often deals with anxiety and mistrust. How it deals with anxiety and mistrust is written below. When you are talking to someone who has anxiety or mistrust in their body language, there are certain things that you can do to try and reassure them.

- The first thing is to make direct eye contact with them and give a firm handshake. You want to be confident and trust who you are saying to understand your position.
- The second thing you can do is verbally reassure the person that you are not trying to harm or cause any emotional or physical damage. Try to explain to them that you intend to communicate only, and that you won't attack them.
- You can also de-stress by smiling and laughing frequently or talking about yourself on a topic

about which you are knowledgeable. It will almost certainly make the conversation flow, since it demonstrates to the other person that you want to talk to them and are interested in making friends with them.

Face-To-Face Communication Relies On Seven Channels Of Nonverbal Communication

Eye contact is the most basic nonverbal expression. It indicates attention, interest, and participation in a conversation. Lack of eye contact can indicate a lack of trust, interest, or confidence in what one is saying, or attempting to control or dominate the conversation.

It may be considered rude in the workplace because it makes those who don't look away feel uncomfortable or insecure about what is being said (and not being said). As with all other forms of nonverbal communication, use only as much eye contact as needed for clarity of message or personal preference.

Non-verbal communication deals with anxiety and mistrust, and understating its cues is important to understand each other.

CHAPTER 15: INCREASING ATTACHMENT

Every connection has some level of attachment. People are more prone to leave a relationship when there is no attachment. People who are not very devoted to their partners are more prone to cheat on them. If a person in a relationship fears that their spouse will abandon them, they are much more likely to cheat on them. Attachment operates in both directions.

One way to make someone more attached to you is to have more good qualities than the existing connection. The higher your quality is in comparison to your spouse, the less likely they are to want to cheat on their relationship and damage themselves in the process.

Another strategy to enhance connection in a relationship is to avoid paying too much attention to the other person. What exactly do I mean by this? If you're constantly not present when the other person wants or needs you, they'll want and need you even more. This is because people crave something they can't have most of the time, making it all the more special when they receive it.

People frequently mix up attachment with love and passion. Attachments are distinct from these sentiments due to their depth and power. Attachments significantly influence our relationships and our ability to achieve happiness. When you have a deep commitment to someone, you will fight for them, be faithful to them, and be there for them through thick and thin. They help you feel secure, safe, cared for, and cherished.

As time passes in a relationship, one or both partners will experience some form of shift; they may start feeling underappreciated or less attracted to their spouse. Most people in this scenario spend some time apart from their spouse out of fear of losing or being dismissed by them, but that's not how you should behave if you want your relationship to survive. You shouldn't ever stop fighting for your loved one, since doing so would cause your attachment to dissolve and your relationship to suffer.

Difference Between Positive And Negative Attachment

There is a difference between positive and negative connections. When individuals have an excellent attachment to someone, they are inclined to help that person in their time of need. This person might be a lover, a friend, or even a parent. Positive connection is associated with health advantages such as enhanced immunological function, reduced blood pressure, and lower stress hormone levels. On the other hand, toxic relationships that are built on fear and hate are known as negative attachments. Insecure people may form negative attachments to family members or friends, not just because they do not love them, but because they are afraid of being ignored.

Fear of abandonment can lead to offensive behavior, and those who suffer from it can go to great lengths to keep others close to them. To overcome insecurity, the person suffering from it must understand that the person to whom they are linked will not desert them.

This is especially true if the individual only has one or two close friends or family members. They may believe that if their one "best friend" quits, no one else would care for them; therefore, their fear prevents them from ending the connection if it happens again with another family member or friend.

The primary distinction between a good and negative attachment is that the person linked to us constantly satisfies our desires for closeness and security in a positive way. The individual related to us regularly breaches or ignores our desire for intimacy and security when we have a bad connection. In a safe relationship, your partner meets all of your requirements, but some of your needs are addressed in an insecure relationship while others are disregarded or abused.

Attachment And Strength Of Relationships

The more valuable time you put in with your spouse, the more satisfied you will be with your relationship and the stronger it will be. When it comes to forming a solid link between two individuals who love one other, time is of the essence.

We must study and comprehend the process of developing these sorts of connections to create and preserve them.

I've found five steps that can help you build healthy, loving relationships:

1. Being able to embrace someone unconditionally is the first step in developing a love connection. By definition, if you can accomplish this, you must unconditionally love yourself. When you aren't there yet, you must focus on accepting yourself before expecting anybody else to love you for who you are.
2. Loving relationships necessitate that we are mindful of our wants; otherwise, we would find it challenging to address the needs of others. How can you possibly know what other people need if you don't know your own needs?

TIP: Make quality time with your partner a part of your everyday routine. Even if you are busy during the week, set out an hour or two on the weekend for the two of you. Avoid arranging other events during that time so that you can concentrate exclusively on each other. If you can't do it at home, go out and do something lovely together.

Genuine loving relationships are built on trust and love rather than fear or intimidation. A spouse who lives in "fear" of not being good enough or losing you will constantly feel uneasy and will never be able to enjoy themselves.

So, how can you show your lover that they are appreciated and that you love them every day? You may do so much for them, but it's not always enough because there's always something more essential happening in their lives such as job, family, friends, and so on.

The essential aspect of determining what makes your spouse happy is to show them what makes them feel good without feeling like a burden, and never causing them to feel obligated to do more for you in return.

Ways To Increase Attachment

Did you know that there are several methods for increasing connection in a relationship to decrease general anxiety? The strength of your connection has a significant impact on the quality of your relationships. You will feel comfortable and secure if you have a solid link with your partner.

Being in a healthy relationship does not need you to lose yourself in it. You may still be an individual with your own personality and hobbies while also connecting with others.

Here are some suggestions for increasing the connection in a relationship:

1. Love and devotion can be expressed with words. The majority of people want to know that they are cared for and loved. Not all of them, though, would say it aloud. They may believe that utilizing such sentences may come across as corny. However, expressing your love and caring for the person you're with through words is the most efficient way to convey how much you care.

2. When it comes to presenting gifts, be inventive. Giving presents does not necessarily involve tangible items such as clothing, accessories, electronics, and home appliances. Simple gestures may often mean more than large gifts, mainly if they originate from the heart. When presenting presents, be imaginative; this will add more significance to your actions.

3. There will inevitably be disputes and conflicts that do not end well in every relationship. Don't

allow these things to bother you for the rest of your life; forgive each other, forget what occurred, and get on with your lives. Holding grudges may make your relationship stressful, resulting in distance between you two.

CHAPTER 16: OVERCOMING POSSESSIVENESS AND JEALOUSY

Every relationship has a high point and a low point. Even if this is correct, the connection is not always up and running. There are various reasons people get jealous and possessive in a relationship, which we shall investigate below.

The difficulty of sharing your spouse with another person or the rest of the world is standard, and can occur even if you adore them dearly. However, it becomes an issue when you cannot manage your emotions and when you allow jealousy to influence your partner's actions.

Jealousy is not necessarily a terrible thing, because it demonstrates how much you care for others. It is also usual for people to show their love for their partners by being overprotective or desiring to spend as much time as possible with them. These are some of the most prevalent symptoms that someone in a relationship is jealous and possessive. Both of these emotions give rise to anxiety in the relationship.

You are being excessively possessive when your relationship causes you to feel like a prisoner. You begin to believe that your spouse should have no life outside of the relationship because whenever they go out with their family or friends, it appears that they are abandoning and ignoring you. If this sounds similar, it is time for some introspection and discussion with your spouse about how much independence you require to feel safe in the relationship.

Psychology of Jealousy And Possessiveness

Jealousy is frequently an indication of insecurity or a suspicion that your partner is cheating on you.

Every human being has a fundamental yearning for security. We want to know that our spouse will be there for us and go to any length to ensure that our connection remains strong.

Knowing that your spouse is trustworthy and loyal will make you feel safer in the relationship.

One of the most challenging things of being in a relationship is dealing with jealousy and possessiveness. The fear of losing your mate is one of the most powerful human emotions, and when there is jealousy and possessiveness towards you, it may seem like a horrific nightmare.

Understanding why your significant other thinks this way will assist you in resolving the situation. There are several reasons why someone may be jealous and possessive in a relationship, but the underlying cause is frequently poor self-esteem or insecurities. It is frequently the result of a childhood experience of being bullied or mistreated by a parent or sibling.

Overcome Complexes And Fearfulness

Somewhere deep inside our subconscious minds, we believe that love is a gift that must be earned. We consider ourselves "fortunate" to have found someone to love and settle down with, and we strive to avoid doing anything that would endanger our prospects of receiving a return on our investment.

How do you get over the complexities and fears that come with falling in love?

Here are three easy tips to prevent you being too passive in your relationship and decrease anxiety:

Don't Think Of Love As A Reward

Humans are creatures of habit; we do familiar and comfortable things to us. When you're with someone you care about, it's easy to fall into the habit of doing whatever pleases her. Isn't that what she wants, after all? You want to know how to make her happy, so you'll hit all of the perfect notes and say everything she needs to hear.

The reality is that if you do not think for yourself and concentrate on your own needs occasionally — even if it means disappointing her — there's no actual emotional link between the two of you.

Try Not To Be Too Charming

A certain element of mystery is required for charm. There is no charm if everything goes according to plan, because everything is always under control. It indicates that you should prepare for unavoidable blunders and catastrophes — events that don't go as planned but make you look excellent in the eyes of your partner.

Heal Trust Issues

Trust is a potent force. It's the glue that holds many relationships together and allows people to form intimate friendships. However, it can be challenging to repair once broken. If your partner betrays you with someone you care about, or if lying or adultery has brought your relationship to its knees, it's difficult to regain trust in them.

Attempting to fix trust issues in a relationship is difficult, but taking action is sometimes the best way to do it. The most common error individuals make when attempting to restore a relationship after a betrayal is trying to prevent getting hurt again, rather than determining what occurred in the first place. Accept no excuses such as, "He/she didn't mean it," or, "It'll never happen again." For a relationship to succeed, both partners must feel safe and trusting.

If you wish to mend trust issues in a relationship, try the following:

Find The Root of The Issue

When a person is in love, they desire to spend all their time with their spouse. Sometimes people get envious, which leads to possessiveness. This type of behavior frequently has a significant impact on both spouses' lives and might hurt them. Suppose you feel this way about your spouse; attempt to identify the source of the problem which is causing you to feel this way. Then strive to make a permanent alteration.

Here are some suggestions to assist you to overcome this feeling:

- Learn when to trust your spouse; it's difficult, but try not to be too concerned if they leave home or don't respond to phone calls or text messages right away.
- Think before acting; attempt to comprehend other people's perspectives and not leap to conclusions.

- Communicate with your spouse; it is preferable to fix difficulties as soon as possible rather than deal with them later.
- Give your spouse some space; don't check their cellphone every 10 minutes and be patient and respectful of their privacy.

Develop Realistic Expectations

Unrealistic expectations fuel jealousy and possessiveness. Unless you've been together for an extended period, you may assume that your spouse will always be there for you. But that's not a realistic option. You can't always rely on someone to be present when you need them to be. You also can't bet on the relationship staying as it is today indefinitely.

Trying to do both puts you at risk of failing. However, if you're realistic about what you want from a relationship and how long it's likely to continue, you'll avoid splitting up over petty concerns when serious problems develop.

Having realistic expectations in a relationship might help you get closer to your spouse and more fulfilled as a person. When you are possessive in a relationship, the other person does not feel pleased; instead, they feel smothered and confined. To overcome jealousy, you must recognize that none of you has exclusive control over the other's life. It may be difficult when you see your spouse spending valuable time with someone else but consider the benefits they can gain from this encounter, such as new career opportunities.

Show Gratitude

Being appreciative in a relationship is complicated. It may be time-consuming, unpleasant, and just brutal. However, like any other ability, thankfulness in a relationship can be honed with practice.

Gratitude is a terrific technique to go deeper in a relationship. There are a variety of ways to show gratitude in order to benefit a relationship. Couples, for example, are happier with their relationship after expressing thanks to one another.

When expressing thanks, the key is to be honest and explicit. You care when you say things like, "Thank you for always being there for me," or, "You're very thoughtful."

Don't be afraid to express your gratitude to your mate! Here are some examples of how to do so:

1. Make it a habit to express gratitude aloud five times every day. It will assist in instilling a sense of appreciation and thankfulness in your relationship daily.
2. Express gratitude when anything remarkable occurs. Say thank you and tell them what they did that was so lovely when your spouse does something kind for you, such as picking up the dry cleaning or mowing the grass. It will make your spouse feel recognized and valued for their work.

Accept Yourself

In a relationship, accept yourself. It is critical to accept the aspects of your spouse that you dislike and accept yourself. If you can't take some parts of yourself, you won't get people for who they are. Trying to transform someone into someone else will never succeed, and it will only result in bitterness.

I've had to examine and change undesirable behaviors in my own life numerous times, but how can I expect others to do so if I can't?

So that you can expect the same from another person, you must be prepared to accept things about yourself and focus on fixing them. Acceptance is the first step in making improvements. If you don't acknowledge anything, you won't be able to work on it or even notice an issue.

It's good to be yourself in a relationship, as long as you and your spouse both recognize that you need time apart from time to time. Your spouse must come to understand and appreciate your desire for privacy. If they can't provide it to you and constantly attempt to control you, they might not be the ideal person for you. You must accept them and allow them to be who they are. So, don't compare them to anybody else or even to yourself, because everyone is unique.

How Can You Treat The Possessiveness Of Your Partner?

There is no disputing that your partner's possessiveness may be aggravating. However, you must step carefully to preserve harmony in your relationship. Here are some things you may do to maintain the peace and show love and compassion to your possessive partner:

Respect Your Spouse

One of the sweetest things you could do for a jealous person is to express your gratitude. Very jealous people may worry that their partner does not value them enough. It might be because they are uneasy about themselves and they expect their partners to be the same. If this is the case with your relationship, try to express how much you appreciate them and how important they are. It will make them feel better about themselves and prevent them from being overly possessive or insecure.

Use Caution

While it's natural for anybody to feel a tiny bit jealous sometimes, it's critical not to allow envy to rule your life or relationship. If your lover is very jealous, learn not to take it personally. Jealousy is frequently a sign of insecurity and self-doubt, so handling it as such may help you and your spouse put things in perspective.

You can deal with all the tensions and anxiety in your relationship if you succeed at treating these negative emotions.

CHAPTER 17: TRUST IN A RELATIONSHIP

The quality of the interpersonal connection between persons is characterized as trust in a relationship. Along with commitment and intimacy, it is one of the three critical components of closeness in partnerships. A personality trait determines how individuals act in a trusting relationship and can have severe ramifications for their well-being. You can prevent anxiety from building up if there is trust between you and your partner.

Temptation is a factor that helps develop trust in a relationship. Roy F. Baumeister, a social psychologist, has examined the topic of temptation, arguing that people have a finite quantity of willpower and self-discipline. That is why developing trust in a relationship is critical since, without it, people will lack self-control and are more prone to succumb to temptations.

Communication is another crucial component that influences trust in a relationship. Communicating with your spouse can help you understand them better and feel closer to them, all of which contribute to developing confidence in a relationship.

Trust difficulties arise in relationships when people take things for granted and do not believe what their partners say. When this occurs, it is normal for that individual to begin doubting their partner's love for them.

So, how can we address the issue of trust concerns in relationships? Trust does not develop quickly, but it may happen if the individuals involved are prepared to take a chance and stop doubting each other's love for them. Being truthful and honest is essential for resolving trust difficulties in partnerships. If a person begins to lie or hide facts from their spouse, they will never rebuild trust with that person again.

The Importance Of Trust

Trust is crucial in all relationships, especially romantic ones. Honesty, openness, and communication are the foundations of trust. Building and restoring confidence takes time, but the work is worthwhile.

Trust is more than simply a concept or a belief; it is an emotional bond between two people that allows them to feel secure being vulnerable in the presence of each other. Trust must be developed on a foundation of love and mutual respect.

Communication is crucial in every relationship; however, without trust, communication will only go so far, since there will always be an undertone of dread and doubt flowing underneath the surface of the dialogue. Communication can help you achieve an agreement, but it cannot address deep-seated worries and questions about whether your spouse is who he claims to be or if he loves you for who you are.

While there is no magic recipe for establishing or reestablishing trust, there are several actions you can take to make the process go more smoothly.

Step 1: Be truthful with your spouse. If you've previously lost trust by harboring secrets, try being more upfront about your emotions and behaviors. Being upfront will assist you in developing confidence in the future.

Trust cannot exist in a loving relationship unless there is honesty. Honesty is essential in any relationship, especially a loving partnership.

Step 2: Allow your spouse to express their worries without getting defensive. Listen closely to what your spouse says and let them draw their own judgments about the situation. Agree with your spouse until you've heard what they have to say. Instead of protecting yourself, try questioning them about how they feel and why they think the way they do. Because your spouse will feel accepted and valued, this will enhance your relationship.

Trust cannot exist in a loving relationship unless there is honesty.

The Meaning Of Trust In A Relationship

The concept of what is meant by the term trust remains unclear. The word comes from combining "truth" and "faith."

Whether or not a person can be trusted is a complicated process that requires various abilities and traits. It is much more than having one's intentions verified by the other person's acts. Trust is the ability to put faith in another person's ideals and viewpoints, even if they differ from one's own. As a result, trust in a relationship has quite different meanings for men and women.

Trust in relationships does not come naturally; instead, it must be earned through experience and the comprehension of other people's characteristics. The capacity to trust is dependent on the level of communication between partners. This means that any issues must be treated freely and without judgment or defensiveness. To feel comfortable and secure enough to disclose your exact wishes and anxieties, you must have faith.

When there is love, there will always be trust. We go to great lengths for individuals we care about because we love them. Not only do we provide for them, but we also guarantee them that they will never be left alone or abandoned.

Their delight is also our happiness. We will do anything to put a smile on our partner's face and make them feel safe in this world. Undying love is the definition of trust in a loving relationship.

Ways To Build Trust

Building trust is essential for a healthy relationship and can be accomplished in various ways. The most crucial point is that it takes time to build trust. Don't anticipate your significant other to trust you straight away; trust takes time to develop.

Here are some pointers on how to foster trust in a love relationship:

Respectfully Treat Your Spouse

When attempting to create trust in a relationship, it is critical to demonstrate your love for your spouse and respect for them. When you treat your spouse with dignity, they are more inclined to trust you.

Be Truthful With Your Partner

If either person does not feel entirely comfortable being honest, it is understandable if the other person does not believe they can genuinely trust them. It's critical for both partners in a relationship to feel safe enough to share their thoughts and ideas without fear of being judged.

Participate In Your Partner's Hobbies And Interests

When we first begin dating someone, we spend a lot of time figuring out what makes them tick and what they like. However, spending quality time with our partners might become normal after a while, and we may lose sight of its importance.

How Cheating Affects A Relationship

The most significant betrayal in a relationship is known as cheating. According to one poll, most men and women regard adultery as an unforgivable sin in a marriage. Even if you don't want to talk things out with your spouse, adultery does not always indicate the end of the wedding.

To evaluate if adultery is grounds for divorce, you must go beyond the act itself and consider how it impacts you and your relationship.

Finding out your lover has cheated on you is never easy. And the fallout can be even more difficult. Certain characteristics impact the severity of infidelity.

Assume your partner and the person with whom they were dishonest had a great physical or emotional distance. It might not have been as horrible in that scenario as it would have been if they had seen someone in their neighborhood. It's more likely to be an ongoing relationship if they're exchanging personal information and graphic photographs with someone they met on a dating service.

A wide age gap between the cheater and the person with whom they were dishonest indicates that it was most likely an emotional affair. In contrast, cheating with someone close in age suggests that it began due to physical attraction. But bear in mind that this is only relevant if you intend to save the relationship. If you've already decided to leave your spouse, it won't matter whether you remain or depart.

But, you can rebuild the trust if you want to rectify your mistakes.

Restoring The Trust

Trust is the foundation of any relationship. Trust does not grow overnight, but it is possible to rebuild it if both sides try. One of the first stages in establishing trust is acknowledging wrongdoing and being prepared to take the consequences. The following stage is to recover your partner's confidence by demonstrating that you will not repeat the offending conduct.

Once trust has been broken, it may take time for your spouse to feel at ease with you and your relationship again. However, don't expect your partner to forgive you for your error suddenly. Allow time for your spouse to recover from the betrayal, and make sure you're prepared to work on repairing the connection before demanding forgiveness from them.

Recognizing your fault and committing to modifying your conduct to re-establish trust in a relationship may go a long way toward reestablishing trust between you two. Before anticipating a complete reconciliation, be patient with each other and take the time necessary to show your trustworthiness thoroughly.

Tell your spouse to sit down and express your feelings about their acts, your pain, and what they have done to cause you to feel this way. Allow them to apologize and state that they recognize they have done something wrong, and demonstrate that they will not repeat it. Set some goals for when you and your partner will move on from this. If you discuss something more than once, make sure you are both willing to discuss it as many times as necessary until one or both of you can move on from it.

Discover What Caused The Trust To Be Destroyed In The First Place

Trust in a partnership can be shattered when one person fails to maintain their end of the deal. Did they deceive you? Were they unfaithful? Did they do anything that went against your moral standards and sense of right and wrong?

If a lie was told, it is conceivable that the lie was about something else. Perhaps it had something to do with where your partner went last night or what he did earlier this week. Maybe many falsehoods have been uttered, and the issue is that one individual appears to have no integrity at all.

If there was cheating, there might be other flaws as well. Has your partner ever had an affair with one of their coworkers? You must be aware of these facts to resolve the issue and restore trust in your relationship.

If there was some form of betrayal, whether it was because the individual broke the agreement or breached your moral code, then perhaps it is just part of his character. Maybe he's always been untrustworthy, and you simply didn't know it or know what it meant when someone appeared to be honest but wasn't.

Building trust in a relationship reduces anxiety. The more you trust your spouse, the more protected, comfortable, and peaceful you feel. Trust is also an indication of commitment; therefore, developing trust can reduce anxiety in partnerships.

CHAPTER 18: RESOLVING COUPLE'S CONFLICTS

Conflicts can be the cause of anxiety in a relationship. This anxiety may harm the bonds that shape people.

Conflict specifically means oral disagreement or debate. Avoiding marriage conflicts is a tremendous goal. It is a ridiculous claim to think that a happy marriage works on autopilot and that there are no marriage conflicts or disagreements. People sometimes disagree, and that's not necessarily a bad thing; you have the right to have a different opinion than your partner. The important thing is to communicate effectively and soundly in order to understand each other better and strengthen our relationships.

Reasons for Conflicts

There are a lot of reasons that can cause conflict. Manage these disagreements as a team, and let the relationship grow. Do not expect the solution to a problem to happen automatically. Deal with it. Sometimes, you can't simply adjust to a problem. Some of the reasons are:

Unfulfilled and Unrealistic Expectations

Both unfulfilled and sometimes unrealistic expectations often lead to marital discord. One partner shares similar expectations, assuming the other is a mental leader. Frustration comes when things and events do not go as planned. Partners blame spouses for not supporting lifestyle choices, family expectations, household chores, or career choices in the way a dissatisfied spouse envisioned they would.

Lack of Sexual Compatibility

An inconsistent sexual drive, which makes you want to have sex more often than your lesser sexual partner, can drive the difference between you and your partner. Stress in the workplace, housework, skepticism, pressure to date, and a lack of genuine communication about sex are some of the significant and stressful issues that lead to marital discord. As you both grow, you will find that building a solid emotional bond with your spouse and embracing other forms of intimacy is very important when it comes to enjoying sexual intimacy with your partner.

The importance of planning sex and getting weekly dates can't be overrated. Having a good conversation with your spouse helps. Hugging your partner, going through your sexual desires and thoughts, and expressing your sincere efforts to meet your partner's sexual needs establishes sexual intimacy with your spouse.

Mismatched Dynamics

In a relationship, both parties are equal partners. Some couples may have radically mismatched dynamics. If one is a domineering spouse and the other is obedient, the latter will inevitably be the caretaker of the spouse. It leads to annoying accumulations and unfair and unhealthy power play, disbanding the marriage.

Conflict And Couples Anxiety

Conflicts are a predictable part of almost every relationship, which can cause anxiety. That's why it is necessary to find a solution in most cases. It may seem incorrect, but some of you suppress your anger or just go along with it. Some people have thought that by confronting a predator, they create an argument, and that's the reason they prefer to stay quiet. Unfortunately, this is not a long-term solution.

Unsettled arguments can prompt disdain and restless struggles in a relationship. More significantly, continuous clashes can antagonistically influence your well-being and future.

Conflict Resolution Skills for Healthy Relationships

Conflicts are a part of life and relationships with other people, but you don't necessarily have to endanger your relationships. Identifying conflicts and learning to deal with them healthily often strengthens your communication. The method to learn is to improve the resolution skills of conflict.

Recognizing, identifying, and expressing one's emotions, learning how to be a positive listener, and communicating with confidence are skills that help healthily manage relationship conflicts. These are just a part of it. If there is a relationship conflict between you and your partner, here are some specific tips that can make it easier for you to get them done together.

Communicate Your Feelings

The only important part of conflict resolution is knowing what's happening inside your head. There are times when you feel angry, frustrated, or depressed without any reason. Sometimes it feels like others aren't doing what they "should" do, but you're unsure what you want them to do, if that makes sense. Journaling is an effective way to reach out to your feelings, thoughts, and expectations, and communicate better with others. This process can be pretty severe, and psychotherapy can help.

Improve your listening skills

The first step of conflict resolution begins with effective listening; it is how good you are at listening compared to how good you are at presenting yourself. Helping others hear and letting them feel that you understand can be very helpful in resolving conflicts. Frequent listening also enables you to close the gap between you two. It can help you understand where the split is, where it came from, and so on.

If you disagree with your partner, it is vital to take the time to understand not only the feelings of the other person, but also why you understand the feelings of the other person. If you don't consider your partner's suggestions and think about what you think will work, your partner may feel that you are ignoring or disabling them. It can also hinder a productive and efficient solution to a problem.

Unfortunately, lively listening is an ability that now no longer every person knows. Whenever you talk, you think that you are listening to the other person, but in actuality, you compose your following response — wondering how wrong the man or woman is, or doing things on the side. It's also not unusual to be so protecting of and entrenched in your very own attitude that you actually can't pay attention to the opposite man or woman's point of view.

Discussing how you feel, and your needs, is also a factor in resolving disputes. Remember to say clearly and firmly what comes to your mind, without being aggressive or defending others.

Always resist the urge to say "you" when fighting with your partner. Instead of saying, "You did what I hate!" (this can be considered blame), you can clarify how your partner's behavior affected you. You are both responsible for your emotions.

Providing details can also help you and your partner understand the wrong of their actions, especially if they weren't aware of what they were doing. It also gives them the chance to defend themselves and explain their behavior.

The word "I" is proper when talking about how you feel about the situation, but when it's time for you and your partner to act, move to a unified "you." You may feel overwhelmed and lonely when you say, "I need to solve this problem." When you say, "This problem needs to be resolved," it may seem that you are not responsible and are trying to leave all the work to your partner.

Find a Solution

When you have clarified your partner's point of view and understand your own point of view, it is time to find a solution to the dispute. Clear and straightforward answers can come when both parties understand each other's points of view. A simple apology can work wonders. Open communication can draw people closer when a conflict arises because of misunderstandings or a lack of understanding of another person's point of view.

Otherwise, a little more work is needed. If there is conflict over an issue and both people disagree, there are several options. Sometimes you disagree, and sometimes you find a compromise. The vital thing is to try to solve things to understand and respect everyone involved.

Agree to Disagree

Compromise can be a healthy way to deal with conflict in a relationship if you do not use it to avoid conflict.

You may find that differences between you and your partner greatly define who you are as a person. For example, when it comes to tastes, you may find that "disagreement" is the best solution and celebrate the difference.

Coping With Conflict

Relationship anxiety can make you doubt your partner's feelings for you, making you create fake scenarios in your head about them, and analyze their actions and words. It can be exhausting and taint our experience with love and relationships. While it requires time and effort to work through, it is possible.

Effective communication is probably the most critical skill in dealing with conflicts and stress in relationships.

Is Conflict Resolution Important for Healthy Relationships?

Conflicts do not necessarily lead to damage. Once resolved, challenges and disagreements in relationships can drive growth, deeper understanding, better communication, and progress towards goals.

ANXIETY IN RELATIONSHIP

There are four possible consequences of disagreements and resolutions of them:

- The result is good for the first person but not for the second person. It is a win-lose situation. One gets what he wants, while the other remains defeated and may feel hurt, angry, and resentful. Such feelings can lead to further disagreements or appear in other areas of the relationship.
- The result benefits the second person, but not the first. It is similar to the first possible result, except there is still somebody being suppressed or hurt in a relationship (a losing scenario).
- The result is bad for both people. Often, neither wants the opponent to "win," so it results in stubbornness on both sides when neither retreats. It is also harmful to the relationship and ultimately toxic or recurring long-term.
- A couple or partner works towards a similarly informative solution and achieves mutually beneficial results. Neither person is defeated or hurt. Therefore, trust for yourself and trust in relationships will increase.

Undoubtedly, the fourth option is ideal for long-term, healthy partnerships, and avoids the possibility of a descending spiral of relationships. In response to conflicts, mutually beneficial outcomes lead to growth and progress.

CHAPTER 19: DO NOT GET LOST IN A RELATIONSHIP

Love is a sensation that makes people feel beautiful and self-assured. We feel incredibly unique when we are in love, and the world becomes more attractive as a result. Being in love is a wonderful experience. But don't get too caught up in this circumstance, because when you love somebody too much, you lose your identity, personal independence, and hobbies.

It is difficult to evaluate things clearly and make choices if you're in love. You must attempt to remain true to yourself and make decisions based on your personality, rather than the influence of others, because when you love somebody too much, all of your choices will be taken with their best interests in mind instead of yours.

It's easy to become lost in a relationship, but if you do not have self-esteem or trust in yourself, you should work on yourself before entering another romantic connection. Develop your individuality, gain independence from other people's perspectives, and choose what you want out of life.

It's fine to like someone, but don't allow them to affect your personality or make you reliant on them for happiness. Your joy should originate from within.

Never let love stand in the way of achieving what is best for you. For example, if your partner wants to leave their work but you want to stay, love should not prevent you from following them. This might be challenging since some things are not simple to give up for love. Just keep in mind that these compromises will ultimately make you a better person.

A loving relationship implies that two people genuinely care about one another and are dedicated to being there for one another through thick and thin. If you're in a relationship like this, be sure it's better for both of you when making a big move like quitting your job or changing careers completely.

If a relationship makes one individual miserable and the other happy, it is not worth continuing since it will not endure forever. When two individuals intend to be together, they are both pleased in the relationship rather than just one of them being happy.

Stay True To Yourself

We all want to be liked for who we are, not because of what we can accomplish for others. It's a basic notion, yet it appears missing in today's relationships.

Attempting to win somebody over by giving them stuff or even doing things for them to adore you is not the way to build a relationship. Everyone should think that it is critical to be loyal to oneself in a meaningful relationship.

If you want to be true to yourself in a meaningful relationship, find someone who knows your characteristics.

The most difficult aspect of being acquainted with someone is revealing your true identity to another person. It will be difficult to have a successful relationship if you cannot be yourself.

Once you've told your boyfriend or girlfriend who you are, it's up to him or her to accept you for who you are. If they don't appreciate you, they're probably not the right person for you. It's critical to remember that the time you initially started dating isn't the only time the two of you came to know one another. You will keep getting to know each other. If you want your relationship to last, you must spend time getting to know one another.

It's easy to enjoy someone when they're at their best, but it's critical that your significant other likes and loves you for who you are. When they accept every aspect of who you are, even your shortcomings and failures, they will realize how vital and unique they consider you to be. They wish to be around someone who will love them for who they are.

Being honest to yourself might be difficult since relationships need work. You must be honest about your feelings and desires while also allowing your companion to be authentic to themself. Being genuine to yourself entails not manipulating your companion or attempting to convert them into someone they are not. The only way for this to succeed is for partners to communicate openly. Both partners must be genuine and pay close attention when their companion expresses their feelings and wishes.

Being genuine implies being true to yourself. That's not the same as being self-centered. When you are genuine to yourself, you remove the potential of being selfish, since selfishness involves concentrating on what is best for yourself at somebody else's expense.

Live With Your Values

Because each of us has our own set of values, you and your spouse are certain to differ on what's essential. There are, nevertheless, certain universal principles that we all share. For example, it's critical to live your values if you're in a relationship. Since you and your spouse differ in behavior, it's an opportunity to develop mutual respect.

However, sometimes life forces us to make less-than-ideal decisions, such as dining at home instead of going out, or skipping our favorite TV show to do laundry.

Compromise and adaptability are the foundations of a loving relationship. When you and your spouse are dedicated to living by your values, adjusting becomes a little simpler.

Here are some ways to see if you and your partner are living your values:

Do You Believe You Have The Freedom To Be Yourself?

This form of freedom is necessary for any type of personal development, but it is especially critical for couples who wish to live according to their ideals. And besides, if you feel that you have to compromise who you are to satisfy your spouse, that's a relationship founded on fear, not love.

Do You Feel Comfortable Expressing Yourself?

Nobody who fully lives their ideas can ever be perfectly happy all of the time. However, if you constantly have to tiptoe around your sentiments to prevent getting into a fight or hurting somebody else's feelings, it's a clue that something isn't right. Relationships should be a safe place where it is acceptable, if not required, to express the wide variety of emotions that we all encounter during our lives.

Trust Yourself

Any strong connection is built on trust. And it's not only about believing in your companion; it's also about believing in yourself and your ability to manage anything that comes your way. That trust will see you through the difficult times and keep your relationship strong and blooming. To establish that trust, you must first ensure that you are on the same page regarding values and goals – what is most important to both of you.

That's why it's critical to have an open and honest conversation with your spouse about how you want your relationship to go. Discuss how you see yourselves enjoying the rest of your life together. Discuss how much time you would like to spend around each other if you intend to create a family and how engaged (or not) each of your families will be in your lives together.

Trusting yourself as much as you trust your lover is one method to keep love alive. You must understand that if your loved one causes you anguish, as they will certainly do, there's always another opportunity for forgiveness. For most individuals, the ability to forgive and forget does not come easy; it necessitates a capacity for self-trust that most of us have yet to acquire.

Self-confidence understands that no matter what anybody does or how much someone hurts you, there'll be another chance for love.

Maintaining a romantic relationship needs two major factors: trust and respect. Because trust develops through time, it is critical to begin a relationship properly. Here are some tips for trusting yourself in a relationship:

Pay Attention To Your Instincts

Pay attention if you have a strong feeling about anything. Even though the person you're seeing appears to be the perfect match for you, it's typically best to be safe than sorry. For example, if you suspect anything is wrong with your companion but they assure you that nothing is wrong, be cautious and trust yourself more than your sentiments of love and devotion.

Set Boundaries Because You Believe In Yourself

Setting and sticking to limits for yourself can help you maintain control of your relationship. For example, suppose your friend wants to go out partying with you every evening, but does not want to include your significant other in their activities. You should probably trust their judgment and respond positively to avoid becoming angry at them. If this makes you feel uncomfortable because it upsets your significant other, put yourself first and say no so that they do not feel left out or mistreated.

Seek Growth

It's not about seeing the forest for the trees. It's all about growing in a loving connection with your partner. If you've ever been in a long-term, committed relationship, you know how it can change you into a whole different person.

Neglecting your spouse will do more damage than good. You're probably not aware of it, but several of your behaviors and actions may be badly impacting your relationship. The trick is to recognize these bad behaviors and modify them before it's too late.

Here are a few bad behaviors you should break right now!

Condemning Your Spouse

You must refrain from constantly criticizing your companion since this can result in plenty of issues in the long term. Criticizing will make them feel uneasy and vulnerable, negatively impacting the relationship. There are better approaches to resolving problems than focusing on little details.

Not Performing Chores

Maybe it's because you despise performing chores, or maybe you're too sleepy or too busy... Whatever the cause, your lack of engagement can cause tremendous strain in your relationship. Do your part!

Channel Your Energy Into Building A Relationship

A healthy connection with your spouse may provide you with more happiness, commitment, and security than you could ever imagine.

The greatest method to strengthen your relationship with your spouse is to show them that you care about them and love spending time with them.

This can be accomplished in a variety of ways. You may, for example, prepare a beautiful supper for them, take them on a date, or get them something as simple as roses or chocolate.

Allow your spouse to be themselves and attend to their interests. You want to inspire one another's natural growth while remaining independent individuals. If you constantly give in to their requirements, they will not mature into adults capable of coping on their own when the time arrives.

It is critical to keep a solid relationship with your partner. Relationships need a lot of effort and an attempt to keep the link strong, happy, and smooth over the years that you're together.

Here are some ideas to help you build your relationship:

Speak To One Another

Everywhere, all the time, and about everything. Talk about what you enjoy that irritates you, and make sure you listen when your partner states their point. This will help you better understand your companion and learn what they love and hate.

Spend Time Together

Don't let work or other obligations come among you two since it might ruin your relationship. Decide ahead of time when you're going to have plans, so that you can both stick to them and spend some quality time together.

Discover Mutual Interests

Learn more about one another's hobbies, likes, and dislikes to discover more similar areas that naturally pull both of you together. Learning about each other will allow you to spend time with one another and enjoy every minute of it while in each other's presence.

CONCLUSION

Anxiety in any relationship can have severe implications and create distance between two partners – even to the verge of breaking up. These tensions consume mental peace, and make both partners shut each other out. That is why you need to take serious measures to decrease or eliminate anxiety to save the precious bond you have built over time.

First of all, you need to pinpoint the causes of the distance and anxiety. Then, talk all that out with your partner to resolve these issues. Your effort alone will be enough to decrease the tension to some extent, as you show how much the relationship holds value in your life. Go for therapy, self-meditation, or show familiar gestures to restore trust. As anxiety consumes both partners, all the efforts are worth it when saving your relationship.

Printed in Great Britain
by Amazon